Shapers of Ecumenical Theology Series

Series Editor: Jesudas M. Athyal

ECUMENICAL ADVENTURE

Shapers of Ecumenical Theology Series
Series Editor: Jesudas M. Athyal

ECUMENICAL ADVENTURE

CHARLES C. WEST

FORTRESS PRESS
MINNEAPOLIS

To the Memory of

M. M. Thomas

He was my inspiration and my guide in ecumenical
affairs from 1947 until his death.

CONTENTS

SHAPERS OF ECUMENICAL THEOLOGY
SERIES

While the history of the Modern Ecumenical Movement is often traced back to the World Missionary Conference in Edinburgh in 1910, it has its roots in lay movements such as the Student Christian Movement, the Young Women's Christian Association and the Young Men's Christian Association where Christians from different confessions and denominations came together to pray, study the Bible, and share their concerns on social issues. The Faith and Order and the Life and Work movements arose out of the inspiration of the Edinburgh Conference, which showed the possibility of churches working toward unity on other matters. The World Council of Churches (WCC) was born out of bringing the Faith and Order and Life and Work movements and the Missionary movement together (although the Missionary movement formally joined the WCC later at the WCC New Delhi Assembly in 1961).

From the beginning itself, however, there were individuals and initiatives from all over the world that built up the ecumenical movement. At the Edinburgh Conference, the most pertinent challenges on the need for ecumenism came from the Chinese and Japanese delegates (there were 17 Asians in a 1200-delegates meeting). V. S. Azariah of India addressed the overwhelmingly Western audience and said, "You have given your bodies to be burned. We ask for love, give us *friends*," thus setting in motion a process that would make *oikoumene* truly a movement of the whole inhabited earth.[1] The deliberations at Edinburgh stimulated scholarly interest in non-Western cultures and religions leading to a long process of discussions that continued at the Missionary conferences in Jerusalem (1928), Tambaram (1938), and beyond.

In the decades that followed the Edinburgh Conference, individuals and initiatives from Asia, Africa, Latin America and the

---

[1] For a detailed discussion, see Wesley Ariarajah, "Contribution of Asian Participants to the Edinburgh 1910 Conference" in *Power, Politics and Plurality: Essays by S. Wesley Ariarajah*, ed. Marshal Fernando (Colombo: Ecumenical Institute for Study and Dialogue, 2016), 271-284.

other parts of the world went on to shape the ecumenical movement at various levels. There were also local and regional initiatives that shaped the ecumenical movement such as Base Ecumenism in Latin America, indigenous theologies from Africa, theologies of the marginalized and subaltern people from Asia, the Urban and Rural Mission, Interreligious Dialogue and several such trends from around the world. Underlying all these movements was the theological basis of a common understanding about the unity of the churches around the world and the vision of building up a just and participatory community. As the policy statement of WCC put it, the "ecumenical process which led to the formation of the WCC was not only a response to the gospel imperative of Christian unity. It was also an affirmation of the call to mission and common witness and an expression of common commitment to the search for justice, peace and reconciliation in a chaotic, warring world divided along the lines of race, class and competing national and religious loyalties."[2]

Within this larger context, Fortress Press has undertaken the publication of a series of volumes on the theme, "Shapers of Ecumenical Theology." These books will highlight the ecumenical vision of some of the individuals and initiatives that shaped modern ecumenical theology and introduce readers to the formation and development of ecumenical theology in the twentieth century. Each volume will contain a representative selection of key figures and their writings, cutting-edge commentary, and detailed introductory and concluding articles. The focus here is on a guided study of a selection of some pivotal ecumenical figures and their writings. The series has a broad ecumenical reach and the history of modern ecumenism will be evaluated in the context of postmodernity and postcoloniality. And consequently, these books will not only address the key developments in ecumenical theology during the last century but will also include an emphasis on their implications for our times and for the future. The books are expected to be used as text books, enabling the students to read the original authors of modern ecumenical theology. Throughout, key themes and issues that drove ecumenical reflection in the last century will be addressed in the series.

---

[2] The Policy Statement on "Common Understanding and Vision of the WCC (CUV)" adopted by the Central Committee of the World Council of Churches in September, 1997.

Let me mention three areas where the books in the series will focus on:

Christian Unity

Apart from the Mainline Protestant churches that have traditionally been seen as the primary constituency of ecumenical institutions, modern ecumenical theology was shaped by confessional diversity with an openness to include diversity even where mutual differences seemed profound. In this context, the Orthodox confession should perhaps be mentioned first, as fellowship with the Orthodox churches contributed immensely to the self-understanding of the ecumenical movement. Most of the Eastern Orthodox churches that had not joined the WCC in the beginning became part of the Council at the New Delhi Assembly. Even before the Assembly, there were discussions to revise the basis of WCC. In response to the demand of the Eastern Orthodox churches, the christocentric affirmation in the basis was revised and set in a Trinitarian setting. The New Delhi Assembly also set in motion a long term study on the theological questions involved in the full integration of the Orthodox communion in the WCC. "Recognizing the central importance given in the Orthodox tradition to the conciliar process in the church of the early centuries, the assembly recommended that a study be undertaken of the councils of the early church and their significance for the ecumenical movement."[3]

Another major Christian group, the Pentecostals too contributed tremendously to shaping ecumenical theology, especially at the grassroots level and among the most vulnerable sections in Asia, Africa and Latin America where Pentecostalism has experienced a vigorous growth. The Joint Consultative Group between Pentecostals and the WCC "determined that a study of discipleship and formation would allow the group to move from a convergence agenda—addressing the nature of the church—to a learning agenda

---

[3] "Orthodox Contribution to the WCC," public lecture by Rev. Dr. Konrad Raiser at an international symposium on "Orthodox Theology and the Future of Ecumenical Dialogue: Perspectives and Problems," June 3, 2003 at Thessaloniki, Greece, accessed March 6, 2018, http://www.oikoumene.org/en/resources/documents/wcc-programmes/ecumenical-movement-in-the-21st-century/member-churches/special-commission-on-participation-of-orthodox-churches/orthodox-contribution-to-the-wcc

in which an exchange of models can strengthen the churches' witness in the world."[4]

The shared vision of ecumenism between the Roman Catholic Church (RCC) and the member churches of WCC too "continues to engage churches and others everywhere in concrete action through its Pilgrimage of Justice and Peace."[5] A Joint Working Group of the WCC and the Vatican was established to monitor, further and promote the relationship and cooperation between the RCC and the WCC and its member churches. In more recent times, Pope Francis, with his deep sensitivity toward environmental threats and critical views on the international economic order and the plight of the refugees, immigrants and the poor, has emerged as a willing partner of the ecumenical movement in reshaping the parameters of Christian unity and witness.

There can thus be little doubt that the ecumenical movement, a global effort to realize the biblical vision of the one body of Christ, has been one of the most important developments in Christianity over the past hundred years. Thanks to the ecumenical vision, Catholic, Orthodox, Protestant, and Pentecostal Christians now make common witness to Christ in various parts of the world. Issues that once caused tension among the Christians has been resolved through dialogue. Participation in the ecumenical movement has also helped churches of different traditions and cultures to forge a broad commitment to reject racism, to stand in solidarity with the poor and the marginalized, to care for the environment, and to strive together for peace. Underlying all this ecumenical endeavor was the vision that the quest for unity is God's will, that has a universal dimension and embraces the human community and all of God's creation. "Church unity is vital to the health of the church and to the future of the human family."[6] Integral to Christian unity is a deep commitment for justice. A commitment to the unity and renewal of the church needs to be held together with an absolute commitment to the reconciliation of God's world. As Philip Potter put it in his 1977 address to the WCC central committee: "The

----

[4] "WCC and Pentecostals Discuss Discipleship and Formation in California," April 11, 2017, accessed March 6, 2018, https://www.oikoumene.org/en/press-centre/news/wcc-and-pentecostals-discuss-discipleship-and-formation-in-california.

[5] "Pope Francis to Visit World Council of Churches this Summer," March 2, 2018, accessed March 6, 2018, http://www.oikoumene.org/en/press-centre/news/pope-francis-to-visit-the-world-council-of-churches-this-summer.

[6] The Policy Statement, "Common Understanding and Vision of the WCC."

whole burden of the ecumenical movement is to cooperate with God in making the *oikoumene* an *oikos*, a home, a family of men and women, of young and old, of varied gifts, cultures, possibilities, where openness, trust, love and justice reign."[7]

Perspectives from the South

Beyond the confessional unity of the churches and an acknowledgment of God's work in the world, the books in this series will also recognize the shifting center of gravity of world Christianity to the Global South. We will include here the pioneering role played by the ecumenical movement in challenging a euro-centric theology and ecclesiology by highlighting the perspectives of the colonized and marginalized people in Asia, Africa and Latin America. In particular, this series will recognize the pivotal role played by the liberation struggles of the oppressed people in shaping ecumenical theology during the last one hundred years. Although Base Ecumenism, as the "ecumenism of the people," originated in Latin America, it has had important ramifications in other parts of the world as well. As Raimundo Barreto puts it, "base ecumenism has not only been an important force transforming and revitalizing interchurch and interfaith relations, but it also offers fresh notions of ecumenicity, which are particularly relevant to recent scholarly attempts to re-examine ecumenical relations in the era of world Christianity."[8]

There were also other grassroots level theological initiatives that played a role in the shaping of ecumenical theology. Among theological initiatives that emerged from Asia, Dalit theology contributed considerably to this process. Dalit theology emerged from the conviction that traditional Christian theology was largely based on the perspectives of the dominant class and caste and consequently did not represent the life situations of the marginalized communities such as the Dalits. "This non-representative character of traditional theology raised serious questions about the credibility of

---

[7] John Briggs, Mercy Amba Oduyoye and Georges Tsetsis, eds., *A History of the Ecumenical Movement Volume 3: 1968-2000* (Geneva: WCC Publications, 2004), 53.

[8] Raimundo C. Barreto Jr., "Base Ecumenism: Latin American Contributions to Ecumenical Praxis and Theory" (Unpublished, April 18, 2016), 2.

the Christian faith when the Indian Church itself became predominantly Dalit in membership."[9]

With one in every four Christians living in sub-Saharan Africa and with a rediscovery of the significance of indigenous African religions and spirituality in the life of the church, the role of the religions and cultures of that continent for the Christian world is being widely recognized. There are also the realities of indigenous ecumenical theological expressions, such as Minjung theology from Korea, Burakumin theologies from Japan, the many womanist theologies, the theology of struggle from the Philippines, homeland theology from Taiwan and so on. The Fortress series will recognize the fundamental paradigm shift in the ecumenical agenda from a decisively non-Western perspective.

These books will therefore recognize a growing interest in viewing ecumenical theology from the perspective of the Global South. In particular, they will examine the impact of selected ecumenical theologians on theological formation through a focus on their life and work and a detailed review of their thought as expressions of ecumenical theological engagement with unity and justice. The underlying concern here is that theologizing in Asia, Africa and Latin America occurs in a context of multi-religiosity on the one hand, and rampant poverty and social inequality on the other and therefore, religiosity and a commitment for justice and peace have been at the center of the ecumenical theology that emerged there.

Theologizing from the Margins

Ecumenism, however, is not something that happens inside the churches, but it is about responsible action with regard to "the whole inhabited earth." From the beginning, the ecumenical movement has been affirming that unity is in the struggle for justice. It was the recognition that ecumenism demands a quest for the realization of justice for the sake of unity; it ties together faith and justice. One significant concept of modern ecumenical theology, therefore, was the perspective from the margins. The marginalized are those people who are pushed out of the mainstream to the periphery—those sidelined in the social, political, cultural and

---

[9] Jesudas M. Athyal, "The Changing Face of the Indian Society, and the New Challenges for Dalit Theology," Paper presented at the International Consultation on, "Dalit Theology and A Theology of the Oppressed" Gurukul Lutheran Theological College, Chennai, November 2004. (Unpublished).

religious life of the mainstream society. Ecumenism is a search for the people in the margins, for the most vulnerable sections of the society. As D. T. Niles put it, "the ecumenical vision revealed indeed God's pilgrim people on the center and frontier of the church and the world."[10]

This series of books also recognizes that ecumenical theology will be prophetic in form and content. Prophetic ecumenism will contain both the powerful word to unmask situations of injustice and the powerful word to announce what is possible. "Ecumenism should bear witness to this word, as a sign of resistance and at the same time as anticipation of what is hoped. The ecumenical movement can never be silent; bold words are an integral part of ecumenism. The attempt to arrive at consensus can turn to be an abdication of the prophetic duty."[11] These books, we hope, will portray ecumenical theology as the message that will unmask situations of injustice and affirm the message of unity and peace.

Charles C. West: Shaper of Ecumenical Theology

It is in this historical and theological background that Fortress Press has initiated the publication of a series of volumes on the theme, "Shapers of Ecumenical Theology." These timely books will highlight the ecumenical vision of key leaders in the movement and suggest its relevance for the contemporary church. Each volume will include a biographical introduction and cutting-edge commentary by well-known scholars in the field; but at the heart of each volume will be significant selections from the writings of the leader under discussion. Since so much scholarly attention has been given to theologians from North Atlantic countries, this series will emphasize theological voices from other parts of the world.

We are happy to publish in this series the "Ecumenical Adventure" of Charles C. West. As a missionary in China in the 1940s, a participant in the ecumenical discussions in Europe that led to the founding of the World Council of Churches and a professor of Christian Ethics for thirty long years, his life spanned the greater part of the twentieth century. He was a contemporary of Reinhold Niebuhr, Karl Barth and Dietrich Bonhoeffer and was

---

[10] Ninan Koshy, *A History of the Ecumenical Movement in Asia, Vol. I* (Hong Kong: CCA, APAY, WSCFAP, 2004), 30.

[11] Ninan Koshy, "Ecumenism: Perspectives from the Margins" (Unpublished, September 8, 2015), 4.

one of the pioneer interpreters of the significance of Marxism for Christian theology. As Keith Clements puts it in the Foreword to the book, West remains essentially a theologian of the *oikoumene*, the whole inhabited earth.

As this book is being published, let me acknowledge the support of the Fortress Press team, particularly, Tim Blevins and Will Bergkamp, in this venture. Fortress Press hopes to partner with ecumenical institutions and publishing houses in a wide range of countries so that the books in this series will be available to people around the world at a locally affordable price. The series will serve as introductory readers providing a great opportunity for scholars, pastors, students and lay Christians to come in contact with first hand texts of the pioneers of ecumenical theology. It is our hope and prayer that this series of books will be received well by ecumenical people around the world.

Jesudas M. Athyal
(Editor of the Series)

ACKNOWLEDGMENTS

This volume reflects my recollections of a lifetime of serving God and the church. I apologize in advance for my lapses in memory regarding dates, locations, statements that were made in passing, and other matters of fact. I offer it not as a work of scholarship but, rather, as a record of how my mission and witness were formed over many decades by my experiences and the people and writings I came to know.

A whole lot of people have helped me in writing these pages. I need to mention my son, Glenn Andrew West, who has collected all my writings and whose estimate of them is undeserved. Any mistakes are mine. I need to mention Kenneth Henke who is my former student and now is archivist for the Princeton Seminary library. I am grateful to Jesudas M. Athyal and his mentor M. M. Thomas who was a lifelong friend and who introduced me to him. I am grateful to my wife, Ruth, who suffered through the last chapter of my book and helped me to complete it, for her companionship over seventy plus years. I have had a full life. I am grateful to Andrew Hagee, who helped me organize my archives, and to Laura Bachmann, who helped me with the last chapter of my memoir, and to all the colleagues in my ministry at Princeton Seminary and World Council of Churches. I should be remiss if I don't mention Johannes Hamel, who influenced my theology and encounter with communism, plus all the persons who were mentioned in my book and had an influence on me. I want to mention George Hunsberger who was co-editor of the book which was my *Festschrift* and was the secretary of the Gospel in Our Culture movement.

Acknowledgment of Previously Published Portions: The article, "Jesus Christ Frees and Unites: Implications for World Peace" was published in *The Princeton Seminary Bulletin*[1]. The article, "Josef Hromadka and the Witness of the Church in East and West Today"

---

[1] Charles C. West, "Jesus Christ Frees and Unites," *The Princeton Seminary Bulletin* LXVII, no.1 (1975): 89-102.

was published in *The Princeton Seminary Bulletin*.[1] Portions from my previously published article, "Community—Christian and Secular" are included in the chapter, "Seminary Years." I wrote the paper, "Community—Christian and Secular" in preparation for the World Conference on Church and Society in 1966. A number of the preparatory essays, including this one, were published under the title, *The Church amid Revolution,* ed. Harvey Cox (New York: Association Press, 1967).

Charles C. West

---

[1] Charles C. West, "Josef Hromadka and the Witness of the Church in East and West Today," *The Princeton Seminary Bulletin* XI, no.1 (1990): 32-45.

FOREWORD

There will be few, if any, readers of this book who cannot remember the moment on September 11, 2001 when the news broke of the terrorist attacks on the Twin Towers in New York and on other sites in the United States. At the Ecumenical Centre in Geneva, one colleague came out of his office and said to me and others, "This is the end of politics." Over the ensuing hours and days the sense of shock vied with horror at the brutal fate of those killed, with outrage at the murderous impulses that had led to killing on such a scale, and with deep alarm and bafflement at the emerging evidence that religious belief had played a major role in motivating the attacks. With real fear, many of us around the world observed how in turn the official response of the US government seemed to be couched only in terms of going to war against ill-defined enemies. It did indeed seem that at the start of the third millennium we were witnessing, if not the end of politics, then at any rate the emergence of a hugely unstable, unpredictable and frightening new world. What did it all mean?

Outbursts of sheer alarm, calls for revenge and counsels of despair were not, however, the only voices heard from the USA. Eight days after the attacks came a letter from Princeton, New Jersey, emailed to friends and colleagues both in the USA and around the world, sounding a clear and distinctive personal note. It called for the events of September 11 to be addressed by people who were prepared to draw on the deepest wells of their faith, humanity and historical wisdom. As horrified and pained as any others at the outrage, as clear as anyone else that this attack carried out by some people of the Muslim world constituted "the most destructive single day in American history," the letter went on to speak of other things: the amazing, spontaneous and often sacrificial help poured out for the victims; the remarkable nationwide turning to prayer by people of all religious traditions; and the danger posed by purely belligerent American rhetoric and actions in return. It was a letter imbued with obvious love for the country that the attackers had sought to harm, but equally a love which, no less, wished to save the country from harming itself.

That letter was written by Charles C. West and his wife Ruth. They went on to ask three questions: How can we learn under God's guidance to live creatively with the insecurity into which we have now been thrust? Can we as a nation learn that we are truly dependent on the community of other nations among whom we live? Can we learn to live with and offer hope to those who resent us and call themselves our enemies? This was a message underwritten both by the Sermon on the Mount and a deeply realistic grasp that the only future for the world lies in finding a way, however difficult, of living beyond resentments and of living together. Two years later, surveying the wreckage of the Western intervention in Iraq, Charles and Ruth issued another letter reflecting on the longer-term and broader challenges facing Western policy-makers on the world stage: "We can only cultivate democracy, freedom and peace. We cannot impose them. They are expressions of a political order that transcends tribe, race, nation and even religion. They reflect in human society the transcendence of God. Because we are sinful, fallible human beings, we must listen to, accommodate to, and live with each other under a common justice that protects our right to profess and proclaim the different ultimate realities in which we believe."

One may well ask, whence came the courage, insight and mature wisdom that could speak so pertinently into that contemporary situation? This book provides the answer: They came out of a whole lifetime of living with the questions thrown up by the never-ending human quest for justice in a world of increasingly rapid social change, and of seeking to interpret *theologically* what is happening in contemporary history. For Charles, the questions have never been purely academic. As a student in the late 1930s New York, he wrestled profoundly to find a personal faith that could give both meaning and energy to his own life, and found it in an apprehension of *grace* as the reality which not only inspires but goes before and beyond all our human endeavors. As a young Presbyterian missionary and teacher in China in the immediate aftermath of World War II, he experienced firsthand the upheavals wrought by the collapse of the old feudal nationalism of that country and the Communist revolution led by Mao-Tse Dong. Soon after, he chose to live in a Europe of bombed cities and disillusioned peoples now rigidly divided between the West and the Soviet-dominated communist East. In Berlin, he came to know pastors and theologians who had known the cost of witnessing for peace and justice under Nazism, including some who had been taught by Dietrich Bonhoeffer and were now seeking to transmit his challenging theology in a Germany and Europe under reconstruction. In turn, he worked for the World Council of Churches (WCC) in Geneva and became part of that gifted team led by W. A. Visser't Hooft, first general secretary of the WCC, and including creative figures like Hendrik Kraemer, Suzanne de Diétrich and Charles' fellow-American Paul Abrecht, pioneers of the new ecumenical way of relating the biblical faith to the realities of the world, not least in matters of peace, racial justice, combating poverty and promoting justice amid rapid social and technological change.

Impelled by his experiences both of China and Eastern Europe, Charles became a major and prophetic interpreter of the significance of Marxism for Christian theology, without ever romantically glossing over the serious issues between them (he had learned too much from Reinhold Niebuhr, Karl Barth and Dietrich Bonhoeffer to allow that to happen). He never lost his deep concern for Europe, especially relations between the East and West during the Cold War, nor for his first love, China and, more widely still, for India and the so-called developing world. Herein lies much of his significance, for while from 1967 to 1992, he was professor of Christian Ethics at Princeton Theological Seminary—one might say the heartland of the Reformed theological tradition in the United States—and has continued at Princeton in retirement, he has remained essentially a theologian of the *oikoumene*, the whole inhabited earth. Living as we do now in a time of forceful isolationist and separatist tendencies both in religion and the world at large, this volume is a precious witness to a very different spirit, of persistence in constructive dialogue for the sake of the common good within and between the peoples and faiths of the world, while rooted in the basal tenet of the Reformed tradition, the grace of God. But to read this book is to see what it means to be a theologian who *lives* by grace. Some twenty years ago I was arrested by his statement in an interview: "Truth does not emerge from winning the argument. It comes from mutual witness."[1] Similar gems

[1] "A Conversation between Ruth and Charles West" in Shin Chiba et al., eds., *Christian Ethics in Ecumenical Context* (Grand Rapids: William B. Eerdmans, 1995), 17.

abound in these pages. May they help to counter the assumption in much of the contemporary public mind that faith is inherently intolerant, sectarian and conflictual.

Hence, Charles not only writes of the recent past and his (with Ruth's) role in it—extraordinarily fascinating in themselves—but witnesses to what is as vitally important today as ever. In so writing, Charles has added yet more to the immense debt already owed him for his contribution to ecumenical life and thought. I hope this memoir will be read and welcomed as a vital encouragement for theology to maintain and strengthen its prophetic calling to interpret what is happening in our history, however fearful that history now appears to be, and to respond by courageous, patient and responsible witness.

With deep gratitude, I now have the honor of commending the volume and its author to a wide readership of seekers after wisdom, for today and tomorrow.

Keith Clements
Former General Secretary
Conference of European Churches
Advent 2017

I. PREPARATION

1. ORIGINS

I was born a participant in history. It has been that way ever since. The date was February 3, 1921, still one month left in the presidency of Woodrow Wilson. It had been a catastrophic few years. Europe had torn itself apart in a world war after a century of relative peace. Empires collapsed. In response to Wilson's ideal, new nations arose claiming freedom and democracy, but also further fragmenting the continent. A vision of world peace that would banish war forever was embodied in the League of Nations. But by 1921, in the United States at least, Wilson was finished. The Senate had rejected his League of Nations. His party had been repudiated at the polls. His successors would be Warren G. Harding and Calvin Coolidge, whose slogan was "return to normalcy" in a world of private enterprise, free of Europe and its problems.

That played itself out in our family as well. My grandfather, after whom I am named, was all his life a stockbroker on Wall Street. In his youth, before the turn of the century, he walked across the Brooklyn Bridge to work each day. He was a man of righteous self-discipline, a deacon in the First Congregational Church, a patron of the Boy Scouts and many other good causes, and, of course, a Republican. My grandmother supported her husband, and raised four children in a spacious, traditional, loving home. My other grandfather made his fortune in cotton merchandising, drawing on contacts from his native North Carolina. They all lived in Montclair, New Jersey, a new suburb of New York in the early twentieth century that was bursting with optimism, energy, and wealth. Leaders of business and finance were among its residents. So were prominent churchmen who led their denominations in world mission. So were social reformers. Harry Emerson Fosdick had his first parish there. In this blend of progressive idealism and traditional enterprise before the First World War, my parents grew up.

The post-war years of my childhood, in Plainfield and Millburn, New Jersey, were quite different. It took ten years to learn that normalcy would not return. It was a turbulent decade, despite the extravagant wealth, the flapper fashions, and the jazz rhythms that buoyed its spirit. The turbulence was expressed in our family as a curious combination of idealistic-confused rebellion and somewhat guilt-laden conformity. This seemed to be the mood of the age as well, at least in our part of the world.

The idealism was expressed politically. My father voted for Al Smith in 1928, and three times for Socialist Party candidate Norman Thomas. ("Par for the course," said Thomas, when Dad met him years later.) The rebellion took the form of books in our library: Sinclair Lewis, Bertrand Russell, and John Dewey among them; and defiance of the laws of Prohibition. I remember gin being made in our bathtub. Traditional lifestyles, enforced by the older generation, were all in question. My mother had defied her father already during World War I by taking an office job. Religiously, too, my parents rebelled. I was baptized at the age of four, but when we moved later, our family never went to church again. I remember my father saying to me that he, as a child, had been forced to go to church and accept its teachings, but he would leave his children free. In adulthood we could decide to be Hindu, Buddhist, Christian, or any other faith of our choice.

Still, the questioning was confused and tinged with guilt. The books did not really lead to a new faith. Alcohol and an extra-marital relation might satisfy but they did not liberate. My mother fell victim to the one, my father to the other, and they lived out their lives with the moral and spiritual confusion, including divorce, into which these ways led them. Yet through it all, they revered God from a distance. In our house the Lord's name was never taken in vain. They loved and cared, as best they could, for their parents and their children.

2. Formation

They sent me, a problem child, to a progressive school, guided by kind teachers and the educational philosophy of John Dewey. There I learned history and math to be sure, but first of all how to be, socially, a human being. There have been many great teachers since, not least my wife, but that was the beginning. I absorbed the nourishing spirit of idealistic humanism. I wanted to believe it. Temperamentally, I hated combat and disliked competition. I was not very good at sports, and life was never, for me, a game. When the game Monopoly came out, I was good at it, but gave it up. I didn't like the feelings—of lust for financial success by bankrupting others, and anxiety lest I go bankrupt—that it aroused in me. Progressive education was not like that. It taught learning by experience in cooperation with others, past and present. A community of persons who develop their capacities in responsible free interaction was its goal.

High school strengthened this spirit. Caring teachers, especially in English and history, broadened our horizons and involved us in the events of our time. The Great Depression leveled everyone, even my stockbroker grandfather, but made us realize that we all, rich and poor, share a common fate and a common hope. The socialism of Eugene Debs and Norman Thomas offered many of us an alluring ideal (we never heard about Karl Marx). But Roosevelt's New Deal also promised a more just and free society, where service to the common good would overcome the lust for private profit. The world situation was, to be sure, fraught with danger. Fascism and Nazism threatened world peace with their brutality and their glorification of war. The Soviet Union, with its Communist ideology and revolutionary practice posed a different challenge. Communist parties around the world shared its goals, served its strategy, and were blind to its oppressions. But surely human goodness and human progress could cope with all of this. I left high school confident that to be a social reformer, probably through the profession of journalism, was the way to work for justice and peace in this challenging world.

Columbia College devastated this confidence. It did so in two ways. On the one hand, Columbia in New York City, in the maelstrom of world events, was more a cosmopolis than a community. In that maelstrom, what group did one join? Where did one find one's friends? Fraternities, with their liquor and sex, reminded me too much of my troubled, broken home. Political groups were clubs concerned more with tactics than ideas. The Debate Society was more interested in winning arguments than in exploring issues. Cynics were everywhere. Where was the humanity? Where were the ideals? I realized much later that cynical bravado was often protective cover for tender idealistic souls, but I was too young to know that then.

On the other hand, Columbia was a center of learning. It introduced its students in their first year to the whole range of Western history: Homer, Aeschylus, Plato, Aristotle, (the Bible was not included), Augustine, and later Descartes, Spinoza, Hume, and Goethe. It opened our minds to realities far deeper than those of Mussolini, Hitler, and Stalin, or even of Franklin Roosevelt, Leon Blum, Neville Chamberlain, or Winston Churchill. Our study of Western history in its political, economic, and philosophical dimensions, from the fall of Rome to the nineteenth century, helped place the twentieth century in perspective. But fundamentally it led, for this student at least, to the question that drove the rest of my study: What meaning, if any, do human existence and human history have? What is the basic reality underlying all things? What does it mean to believe in this reality? If its name is God, who is God? This led me to the one place on campus where the reality of God was taken seriously: the University Christian Association (UCA).

The UCA at Columbia was not closed. All sorts of people, with all kinds of faiths and questions, mine among them, gathered there. Programs on faith and philosophy, international affairs, domestic social problems, and race relations were meat for our meetings. Each year, in an opening retreat, we formulated afresh who we were, and what our purpose was. But all of this was in a context that embraced us all, including the guests who came to speak to us. We could not always understand it, but the reality of God was at work. It was there to be explored, in the world around us and in the response it called for in us. This was what drew us together and gave direction to our meeting. This became my community. It sustained me and made me realize what it means to live by the forgiving grace of God.

Two elements stand out in memory of this experience. The first was discovery that we were part of a world-wide movement of people who lived, who struggled, and who hoped in the God who, in Christ, reigns and redeems the world. Evidence came in from everywhere. The Rev. Jim Robinson came up from Harlem to introduce us to his church, his culture, and to the Christian witness against racism in the United States. T. Z. Koo from China shared with us the joy and the privation of living by faith in Japanese-occupied Shanghai. D. T. Niles of Ceylon (now Sri Lanka) let us know what it was like to be a Christian evangelist in a Buddhist and Hindu land. But most memorable of all was Robert Mackie, the Scot who was general secretary of the World Student Christian Federation. He traveled the world visiting Christian students everywhere, including at Columbia in New York, and wrote his reports in *The Student World*, which he edited. It was a remarkable journal. There he told us about groups in Europe, struggling with the spiritual as well as the physical problems of their nations and their lives, even praying for each other across the battle lines. There were reflections on Christian life—in the French and Dutch resistance, in the army, in prison or in concentration camps, or just in the agony of war. We saw the church in its ecumenical dimensions. It was a vision that captivated us all. In 1940 Mackie reported from a visit to the United States, "There is no country—unless it be China—where the leading students in the Christian movement believe so tenaciously in the world Christian community" (SW xxxiii, 79). So it was with us, leaders and seekers alike.

3. The Faith Question

But something deeper was going on as well: the search for a truth in which one could believe. We were all involved in it. On the one hand, there was the scientific standard of objectivity. To discover truth, one must divest oneself of all that is subjective—attachments, emotions, ambitions, interests—and investigate reality by careful experiments under controlled conditions. Only facts so discovered are true. All the rest (e.g. the arts, morals, religion) is subjective imagination. So we learned in the "natural" sciences: physics, chemistry, biology and geology; and we were invited to use the same method in Psychology, History and Economics as well.

On the other hand, there was a field of conflicting faiths (I use a word here, whose meaning I only discovered later) which competed to engage our subjective lives with meaning and hope. Some of them were not aware of being faiths at all. Their practitioners treated them simply as ways of discovering objective truth by empirical scientific investigation. Yet they were faiths. There was the self-confidence of the physicist, for example, before the atom bomb, of the chemist before pollution of seas and air, of the biologist about the beneficence of natural selection before racism, or of the economist about the laws of the market before the Depression. They all believed in human reason, in human goodness and in human progress, and they lived by that belief.

Some were more realistic, to be sure. Bertrand Russell was clear about the indifference of the universe science was discovering, to all that is human, divine or even moral. "Blind to good and evil, reckless of destruction, omnipotent matter rolls on its relentless way; for man, condemned today to lose his dearest, tomorrow himself to pass through the gate of death, it remains only to cherish, ere yet the blow falls, the lofty thoughts that ennoble his little day; disdaining the coward terrors of the slave of Fate, to worship at the shrine his own hands have built" (*A Free Man's Worship* 1903). One could also go that way. Russell did over a long life, and apparently enjoyed it.

There were also political faiths. The broadest and vaguest of them was "the American way of life." The phrase was coined after World War II but the faith goes far back in history. We lived by it. We fought and some died for it. But what did it mean? The question was deepened by the Great Depression, by revolutionary challenges, and finally by the war itself. It was a time when African-Americans were still being lynched by white vigilantes, and many employers were still paying starvation wages to their workers. What held us together despite our deep divisions of race and class? We knew our enemy. There was general revulsion against Nazism and Fascism, but they were foreign evils. And when the war came to us, we knew what we were fighting against, but what were we fighting for? What ultimate reality underlay our American way of life? What gave it meaning, direction and hope?

There were many answers to that question. Humanist self-assurance was one. It led to many plans for resolving conflict by reason, through economic enterprise, science and technology. It led to cooperative movements that would overcome the social divisions between capital and labor. Many of us wished these people well. We worked with them often, but we did not share their confidence. Could their methods close a concentration camp, stop a lynching, curb strikebreakers, or prevent an armed invasion? Could we believe in human rationality?

On the other side, way over on the left, were the fellow travelers of the Communist Party. They also were humanists, but they understood conflict well. They believed that history is basically a struggle between oppressed, exploited masses of people and their exploiters, a struggle that the masses were already beginning to win, in the revolution that produced the Soviet Union. They knew the USSR was not perfect, but for them it bore the promise of the future, a classless society in which all the means of production would be in the hands of the workers, private capital would be eliminated, each would contribute to the common good according to his or her ability and be rewarded according to his or her need. This was their faith and their hope. It dictated their policy and their actions. They were in every group that worked for social change: in labor unions, in student movements, and even in our Christian Association. We tried to work with them for social reform—those were the days of Popular Fronts on the left—but we learned the hard way that their strategy was to take over, not to cooperate. In the long run, their faith was not ours. We had to define ourselves over against them and resist their dominating tactics, or become fellow travelers ourselves. Struggle was often necessary for justice and human rights, but could one believe in Soviet-led revolution? We could not be that blind, or naïve.

Then there was pacifism: nonviolence as a way of life and as a strategy for overcoming injustice and oppression in human society. Its prophet was of course Mahatma Gandhi, a Hindu, but it had its Christian roots as well, among the Quakers, the Mennonites and the Brethren. This was a different kind of belief. It was personal as well as political. Here was a faith that reached all the way from how one lives one's daily life to a practical philosophy that gives hope to the world. To one who hated coercive militarism as I did, especially when it masqueraded as patriotism, the pacifist way was deeply attractive. I went to Quaker meetings. I read their devotional literature. I saw promise in the victories of Gandhi's movement over the British in India, and in the nonviolent struggles for racial equality and workers' justice here at home. I almost became a principled, conscientious objector to war.

But I never took that step. The reason, finally, was that I could not share the faith. Could one really believe that nonviolent resistance would overcome not only the British in India, but all the other warlike oppressors as well? The League of Nations did not use force when the Japanese invaded Manchuria in 1931, when the Nazis re-armed the Rhineland in 1934, or when Fascist Italy invaded Ethiopia in 1936. The result was the collapse of collective security that led to World War II. Could one accept that? Reinhold Niebuhr wrote an essay in 1940, "Why the Christian Church is not Pacifist." Pacifism, he said, cannot be an historical success story.

Nonviolent methods may be the best tactic in many situations, but they alone cannot be a total strategy for realizing peace and justice. One cannot believe in them. The Peace Churches at their best understand this. They bear their witness to the way of Christ against one powerful evil—the evil of war and violence—and all the wrong it does even while fighting a greater evil. This is a vocational witness. As such, Niebuhr respected it. But it was not every Christian's vocation, and in the end it could not be mine.

4. COMMITMENT

In what, then, could one believe? What is the ultimate reality that governs the universe, and that gives meaning, direction and hope to human history and our lives? How does one choose among all these faiths, and on what basis? If the ultimate reality is God, who or what is God? In the midst of this questioning a book came into my hands, which shed light on all of this. It was *None Other Gods* by W.A. Visser 't Hooft, who, when he wrote it, was general secretary, preceding Robert Mackie, of the World Student Christian Federation. "We must choose," he wrote in the first chapter. In fact, we do choose, whether we admit it or not. But this is not the choice of a product in the market. It is choice of the reality which we trust, to which we commit ourselves, on which we depend, and in the light of which we explore all the other realities of our lives, our universe, and our destinies. It is the choice of faith.

There is a paradox in this choice. On the one hand, it is really a choice. One is free to choose other faiths. One is even free to avoid the question of one's faith altogether, by simply adopting the conventional beliefs of one's environment, or by clothing one's commitments in the language of scientific certainty as the Communists do in their way and many scientists do in theirs. On the other hand, however, one is compelled by faith. It is the compulsion of having found a reality that is true and that requires one to accept and follow it. This truth is not about an object—an atom, a cell or a universe, which one can grasp with the mind, but about a relationship, with others, with nature and with all that is, in which one finds oneself and in which one must live, even if one is a Communist or a scientist or, like Bertrand Russell, an atheist philosopher. We do not control this truth. We cannot prove it or fully define it. We can only explore the inexhaustible mysteries of the relationship; what it means for our lives and for our world, and what response it requires of us.

There are two great dangers in this choice of faith. First, it is a risk. It may be wrong. Reality may not be like that. The believer may be living in an illusory world. He may be pursuing impossible, even destructive, dreams. If so, this wrongness is not just a mistake to be corrected by reasoning; it is a wrong direction of life which calls for conversion. Every believer faces that risk in a world of competing faiths. The question for people of different faiths is not how we find a truth that harmonizes and relativizes all our beliefs, but how we work together on common tasks while witnessing to the ways our faiths influence our approaches to these tasks. In that context conversions may happen. I was an example.

Second, the choice of a faith changes the chooser in ways he or she did not expect. So it happened to me. In a college course on the philosophy of religion, the professor handed a term paper back to me with the comment, "Mr. West has struck a doughty blow for liberal Christianity." Doughty it perhaps was; but it was not successful. I tried hard to harmonize the humanist liberalism in which I was raised with the Christianity I was learning about, but in the long run it did not work. The problem, as I look back on it, was that I was trying to defend myself, my reason and my morality, against the more radical challenge of the Christian gospel. I needed to be converted. Fortunately, it happened gently. Failure as a journalist in the college newspaper broke the vocational illusion with which I came to Columbia. Failure in personal discipline led to utter exhaustion in the senior year. Yet through it all, I was accepted in the community of the Christian Association, and by friends therein. I learned there, in a new way, about the undeserved forgiving grace of God.

It was in this senior year that I made my choice of faith. It was a total choice in the whole above sense. It involved not only ideas, but life. We were surrounded in the Christian Association, by people who lived the Christian faith, both in person and by reports from around the world. But could we believe as they did? Could we find in God who made covenant with the Hebrew people and who came on earth in Jesus Christ, the ultimate reality which gives meaning and direction to our lives as well? Did this God and this Christ make sense in the history of our world? Can one, to cite a skeptical student quoted by Visser 't Hooft, "Hang the whole world on one nail"? Could one trust this relationship to be true, in the sense of faithful, and to guide us into deeper, reliable truth? I remember reading the Gospels—for the first time!—and arguing with Jesus in almost every chapter. Nor did the theology in *The Student World* always help. "Easter: The Victory of a Lost Cause" was the title of one issue. What on earth could that mean?

Still, consider the alternatives. Could one be a Hindu in the way of Gandhi? Could one trust the laws of history, as defined in one way by Adam Smith, or in another way by Karl Marx? Could one trust human reason or human morality to define what is real and good? Could one join the communities that gathered around these various faiths, and try to live by them? Over against them all, I chose to be a Christian.

It was a venture into the unknown. I realized that I had to join a church. I had been baptized as a child, but there was no continuity with that event. My Christian community was the world-wide Student Christian Movement and the Church Universal it represented. That was too general an allegiance, however real it had been for me. So, I went to the Counselor to Protestant Students at Columbia for guidance. "The least self-conscious denomination possible," I said. He sent me to Madison Avenue Presbyterian Church. I have never regretted it. George Buttrick, the preacher, was a stimulating teacher of the faith. The Presbyterian denomination was indeed ecumenical. Its student ministry was through the Student Christian Movement. Its mission led to united churches around the world. Its leaders were among the architects of the World Council of Churches. Never did I hear, from any of them, or from the Madison Avenue pulpit, any emphasis on the distinctiveness of being Presbyterian or Reformed. I was grateful to be a member of a church whose spirit and witness were simply Christian. There, I could explore without human obstacles, the life of faith.

But there was more. The decision to be a Christian was a vocational one as well. If the God whom the Christians worship is true, then I must learn more about this God, and how to see the reality of the world in the light of God's work in it. I must learn how to be God's minister and missionary. That led straight to Union Theological Seminary, then the pre-eminent center in this country of ecumenical encounter and learning.

5. Exploration

Union Theological Seminary was in the profoundest sense an evangelical school. That will surprise many who have given their own meaning to the word "evangelical", but it was true. Christians of all confessions mingled there, but the central mission of the institution was to explore and advocate the Christian faith on every frontier: humanist philosophies and secular disciplines at Columbia University, race and poverty in nearby Harlem, the struggle for justice in society, and the challenges of a world in conflict and ideological turmoil. We understood that we were being prepared for mission on a frontier, whether we served a congregation that called us or founded a new one or went overseas.

First, however, we ourselves had to learn. Of the many teachers who were influential, two, more than any others, shaped my theology and ethics: David Roberts and Reinhold Niebuhr. David Roberts was a philosopher of religion, and a Christian. He wrestled with the relationship. All the problems I had brought with me from Columbia were his as well. He led us through the forest of questions that arise when one tries to figure out the nature of truth about the universe and the meaning of human life within it.

What is ultimate reality and how do we humans understand it? He guided us through the history of philosophy, from Plato to Kant and all the great minds in between, with this question in mind. In other words, Who is God? That was the basic question, though most philosophers didn't put it that way. How can human reason make sense of reality, how is the ultimate conceived?

What is religion and what is its relation to knowledge? We examined other religions—Hinduism, Buddhism, Confucianism, Zoroastrianism and Islam—in their similarities and differences to Christianity as universal claims on human faith and life. We studied various ways to account for religion in terms of other sciences: anthropology, psychology, cultural history and philosophy. Each had a contribution to make in showing how "religious" folk like us behave and why. We were explained psychologically, culturally, historically or in terms of one or another philosophical system, and could learn from all of them. But each of them, in different ways, explained believers in terms of its own structures of rationality. Relation to God was not taken seriously because it was outside those structures. Another faith was assumed here—faith in human reason as the arbiter of all truth, the only way of knowing what is real.

How, then, is truth known? Epistemology the philosophers call it, but it is basic to every way we perceive things and every thought we have. We looked at most of the options on the table at that time: rationalism, empiricism, pragmatism, realism and idealism, as answers to the problem of knowledge, and finally, at the philosophical possibility that truth just might be revealed. It was an amazing, and a liberating insight. It involved a whole new understanding of truth, as the quality of a relationship, not an idea in the mind. It comes to us from another who relates to us and whom we trust, not from our self-centered rationality. Rational concepts, empirical facts, pragmatic policy, realistic analysis and ideal visions have their place but they are relative to and biased by the person who employs them, and the company of his or her peers. Truth—revelation—is the inexhaustible mystery of a relationship to which one responds and which one explores with one's whole life. Whom does one trust—ultimately? That is, one's God.

These thoughts, this theology, has grown over the years, but the ground was plowed and the seeds were planted in David Roberts' classes. If angels are God's messengers, he was one to me.

Reinhold Niebuhr was quite different. He was an activist, driven as I was by opposition to violence and injustice in the world. But in the struggle, he confronted and shook the liberal faith I was trying to maintain. It was a way he himself had traveled, from pacifism to participation in revolutionary struggle, from socialist vision to balance of power in a mixed economy—in short from idealism to realism about human society.

This was rooted in the Reformation faith of his home, his family, and his church. I did not have those roots; I had to sink them with his help. Original sin, he often said, is one Christian doctrine that is empirically verifiable. Human beings have been created good but in their freedom they have become sinners. The will to live becomes the will to power and leads to power structures victimizing the powerless. Enjoyment of God's gifts becomes the desire to possess and leads to vast concentrations of wealth exploiting the poor. Community spirit becomes collective self-assertion which leads to conquest, enslavement and war. In all of this the God of justice and love judges our bias, our pride, our covetousness, and all the ways we justify ourselves against others, while confronting us with the sacrificial love of Jesus Christ. Christians are called to work for a greater relative justice by balancing power with power, while repenting of the harm that even their most responsible actions may do, in ways that will affect their future acts and relations. We are justified by God's forgiveness, not by our own virtue. We are challenged to ever more imaginative justice by the love of God in Christ. In this tension, by faith in this God and with this confident hope, we live. This is Christian ethics.

All this I had to learn, and am still learning, first from Niebuhr, then from other teachers in the faith. But it was Niebuhr who, in his course on the history of ethics, first laid out for us, his students, the whole of world history as the scene of this drama. He led us from the ethics of primitive societies through Egypt, Babylon, the Hebrews, the Greeks, both their dramas and their philosophies, and the Romans, down to the New Testament record of the life, death and resurrection of Christ. Then, as a critical participant, he took us through the whole history of Christian ethics from the time of Christ to the twentieth century. The Old Testament story of God's dealing with the Hebrews was for him a key to the entire history of the Middle East from Egypt to Babylonia and Persia. In all those societies he found the struggle for justice at work, in the power of order, and the rebellion against it, in the establishment of law, and prophetic protest in the name of justice and love. He found the Greek tragic dramatists—Aeschylus and Sophocles in particular—more insightful than the philosophers. They probed the dilemma of humanity more profoundly and did not try to transcend it or cover it over with structures of reason. He wrestled with the message of Jesus in the Gospels and with the faith of Paul—the sources and inspiration of his own faith. I still have one quotation in my notes from that class, commenting on the Pharisee and the publican who went down to the temple to pray: "The world is divided between saints who know they are not saints and sinners who do not know they are sinners." We are saved by mercy, not by our own good actions. Even the redeemed are still sinners, until, in the final judgment, history is fulfilled and ends.

He carried the theme through Christian history. He was critical of conservatives like Clement of Alexandria, who excused inequality of wealth by almsgiving and claims to be "poor in spirit." He understood ascetics who rejected compromise and tried to purge sin by separation and self-denial, but he disliked their body-spirit dualism and their denial of the world. His model for such a witness was Francis of Assisi, who loved the world, but through the selfless purity of Jesus. But Augustine of Hippo, who described the dynamic tension between the "City of God" and the "City of This World" and explored Christian hope and responsibility within it, was his guiding theologian. He found that tension missing in Thomas Aquinas but saw it again in Martin Luther, whose strengths and weaknesses he probed along with that of John Calvin and the many branches of the more radical Reformation. Then he took us into theological dialogue with the ethics of secular philosophies: naturalism, idealism, and even the dialectical materialism of Karl Marx.

There were other great teachers besides Roberts and Niebuhr at Union Seminary in those days. There was John Bennett, the liberal, chastened by Niebuhr, my thesis adviser, to whom I went first with my problems and thoughts. He was the great clarifier and synthesizer whose quiet genius was behind many an ecumenical report on church and society from Oxford 1937 to Thessalonika 1959. There was Paul Tillich, that great synthesizer of theology, philosophy and culture to whom David Roberts once said, "The difference between us is that you can hold all the elements of your system together in your mind and I can't." Tillich protested: "It is not my system. It is reality!" I learned much from his learned vision, but I could never quite find in his system that ultimate reality.

There was also Henry P. van Dusen. He was liberal in theology but a convert to world mission, having visited stations in the Pacific and Asia, so I went to him with my mission vocation and asked where I should go. His answer was unequivocal: the greatest challenge in the mission field was China. He was right, and I went there. Then there was Henry Sloane Coffin, Uncle Henry to all of us, who guided us in relating theology to the daily life of ministry.

They all helped as we students explored our mission in the history that lay before us. But for some of us it was Niebuhr who taught us the poise of Christian action, responding to the grace and judgment of God in the world around us. We have built on it, sometimes in directions that were not his. But he remains over the years, our teacher, our companion and our guide.

6. LIFE AND VOCATION

According to Albert Einstein there are four dimensions of physical reality. The same can be said of human reality—at least of the reality explored here—as well. First, duration, or time, the one he added, becomes, for humans, history. It is the thread of this memoir. The others are not physical but relational. Second is ethics—the living relation to God. Third is mission—bearing witness to God in the world around us. But there is a fourth, more personal dimension as well that gives body to all the others. In the midst of trying to understand the living relation to God which is Christian ethics, and before the first missionary assignment, something else happened to me in that more personal dimension: Ruth came into my life; we married, and our first child was born.

It wasn't planned. It just happened. I wasn't a good catch—thin, gawky, and over serious. I had two brothers but no sister. I had learned from childhood to keep a certain emotional distance from my mother. Though I dated, I did not really know how to relate to young women and I was, frankly, a bit afraid of them. All this was softened by the fellowship of the Christian Association. It was there that I met Ruth. It went deeper, but never hit bottom. Seventy years later I am still exploring the depths of her spirit and discovering new things. It's wonderful.

I was a cheapskate however. Our first date was in the Cloisters, the medieval monastery museum, free entry and a ten cent bus ride up the Hudson River. How serious can a theology student be on a first date with a girl? Second date, we crossed the Hudson on a ferry and climbed the Palisades. The third, we went to the Bronx Zoo. Fourth, we went to the Cherry Lane Theater in Greenwich Village where a rollicking troupe performed Gilbert & Sullivan's, "The Sorcerer." So it went, almost every weekend through the fall. There were meetings and lectures. There must have been a dance or two, though I don't remember them. We were just two people, both emotionally reserved, getting to know each other. I was learning, ever more deeply, how to trust a woman. Then one day she asked me what I was going to do with my life. I don't remember what I said, but the dam broke—and I was swept up in her love. Seventy years later I am still wonderfully unbalanced, living with the flow.

Ruth is the daughter of missionary parents. She spent much of her childhood in China where her father, Dr. Arthur Carson, was a rural sociologist, who worked for years out of Cheeloo University in Shandong, China. Her last two years were in the Philippines when her father became president of Silliman University on the Island of Negros. While she was in college in the United States, World War II broke out in Asia. Her family hid out in the mountains from the Japanese occupation and she did not hear from them for two years. When they came home, we were already engaged. But, they approved and arranged the wedding. It was September 6, 1944. We moved into a dormitory in Union Theological Seminary. We lived on a floor with thirty other couples, all but one of whom had been married that summer.

It was an eventful year in all four dimensions. We applied to, and were accepted by, the Board of Foreign Missions of the Presbyterian Church, to be missionaries in China. Ruth's parents were delighted. Everyone, including Chinese Christians with whom we talked, agreed with Dr. van Dusen that it was the land of the greatest challenge and promise for Christian mission. So we planned. It postponed Ruth's graduation for six months. Finally, at the end of the year, I was granted a fellowship for doctoral study, which had to be taken for the next year or not at all. That was not planned either. Fortunately, the Board of Foreign Missions was understanding. I was ordained by the Presbytery of New York City as a minister in mission in the same month. My mother provided housing, and a friend helped care for the baby so Ruth could finish college. I went off to Yale (came home weekends) to pursue a doctorate in Christian Ethics with H. Richard Niebuhr, Reinhold Niebuhr's brother.

7. Total Immersion

What followed was a year of immersion in a vast sea of philosophy, theology and social theory of all kinds. The sea was not stagnant. It flowed, and its flow was the history of Western civilization. We who navigated it also had an objective. We didn't stop at every port along the way. Our concern was ethics and the faiths that underlay it. How did those who formed our civilization understand the ultimate reality in which human history takes place? What, in their view, is the meaning of human life, its place in the world, and its purpose and its destiny? What have these understandings to teach us about our lives, our faiths, and our hopes today?

I had been prepared for this enterprise by Reinhold Niebuhr's sweeping grasp of the trends of history, evaluating each theologian or philosopher along the way as if he were a contemporary. But Richard Niebuhr was of a different temperament. "Don't make outlines," he said, "of Plato, Aristotle or the Stoics, of the ethics of Moses, Jesus or Paul, of Augustine or Thomas Aquinas, of Luther Calvin Wesley, Hume or Kant. Instead read them, as participants in their world. A great thinker," he once suggested, "is like a crystal; not just to be analyzed but to be appreciated from various angles for a variety of insights and perspectives." So we explored the great minds of Western history, Christian and non-Christian, one by one through the year. I still have the notes. They are full of insights; and they are not outlines.

But Ruth and I had also a special future in mind. We knew we were going to China. Therefore, I added two special fields to my doctoral study. The first was Marxism in the context of social theory in the last two centuries, guided by Dr. Liston Pope. We explored that social theory from its roots in radical Christianity through its revolutionary atheism in Karl Marx to its fruits in the democratic socialism of Europe and quite otherwise in the Soviet Communism of Lenin and Stalin. It was clear that China was headed that way. The Kuomintang (Guomindang) was disintegrating. The only question was what form the revolution would take. How was the judgment and promise of God at work in it? What would be the Christian witness in the midst of it? I was preparing to be part of that quest and that witness with all the knowledge of Marxism I could absorb. Little did I know what would happen in the real work we were about to enter.

The other field of study was the history of Chinese social ethics, from the age of Confucius to the turmoil of the twentieth century, under the benevolent guidance of Dr. Kenneth Scott Latourette, "Uncle Ken" as we call him.

First, a word about Uncle Ken himself. He was a bachelor and lived on the Yale Divinity School campus. Each week, he gathered a group of us in his living room for an evening of what can best be called spiritual reflection. First, each of us in turn described, and discussed with him and the group, our own faith, our questions and the vocation to which we were led. That took the fall term. In the spring we explored Christian doctrines in the same manner, and closed the year with a worship service that drew us all together. Some nine years later, I met him by chance on the campus and remarked that I had just handed in my dissertation. "Oh," he said, "Let me take you to lunch!" Where he had been going, I don't know, but he turned around and led me to the Divinity School dining room. Uncle Ken cared about each of us personally, in our calling and our relation to God. He prayed for and with us. He was our pastor.

As a teacher, he didn't try to shape my perspective. Instead he threw me into the literature of China's classical age (in English translation of course; I couldn't read classical Chinese) and let me sleep. It was another world. I still taste the flavor of it. Like ancient Greece for western society, it was the source of Chinese culture, though unlike the West, it faced no revolutionary revelation. In its Confucian form, that culture molded Chinese civilization for 2000 years. So I learned, about Confucius and his classic books of course, but also about Daoism, that anti-Confucian philosophy that persists as an undercurrent through Chinese history, about Sunzi, the military philosopher who guided warlords, about Legalism, the philosophy of governing all by law that so fascinated the first uniter of all China, Chin Shi Huangdi, about the eleventh century reformer Wang Anshi who was frustrated in his military and flood-control projects by Confucian philosophers, and on down to the twentieth century when everything fell apart under the impact of Western economic, military and technological power.

The twentieth century was a fascinating study. There was wholesale borrowing of Western philosophies and efforts to blend them with the Confucian tradition. There were efforts to appropriate Western science and technology but to keep the substance of tradition intact apart from it. There were revolutionary philosophers like Sun Yat Sen, revered as the father of modern China, and there were political leaders, both Confucian (Chiang Kai-Shek) and Communists who claimed his heritage. China, from 1911 when the Empire fell, to 1949 when the Communists took over, was a cauldron of experiments, movements and ideas trying to redefine and rebuild China. Christians were part of it, including missionaries. Into all this, Uncle Ken, the teacher, led me. It was an exciting prospect. After comprehensive examinations I was ready to go to that country, where Ruth had spent part of her childhood, and my father-in-law had been a missionary.

II. CHINA

1. On the Way

It was a second immersion. Chinese language school had already begun at Yale by the time the doctoral comprehensive examinations were over. From the staggering burden of accounting for all I had learned ("West," remarked Liston Pope dryly, "You know more now than you will ever know again in your life.") I joined Ruth and plunged late into memorizing Chinese sentence patterns, the basis of the spoken language ("The first two thousand are difficult." Our teacher told us, "then the next fifty thousand come easily"). Then, three months later in early 1947, the whole language school moved, and we with it, to Beijing China.

We traveled from San Francisco to Shanghai in the Marine Lynx, a World War II troopship, men in one hold, women and children in another, in three tier canvas bunks. It was chartered by the Mission Boards and was full of missionaries going to China and the Philippines, 325 of us in all. We were a motley crowd. All colors of the spiritual rainbow, except Orthodox and Roman Catholic, were present among us. There was a group of Pentecostals whose tongues resounded from the metal walls of the assembly room amidships. There were faith missionaries of all kinds, and people from Boards connected with splinter churches or no church at all. And in their midst were a few missionaries like us, sent by churches such as the Baptist, Congregational, Episcopal, Lutheran, Methodist, Reformed and Presbyterian who the next year in Amsterdam would join in the great ecumenical enterprise of the twentieth century, the World Council of Churches. We ecumenicals were thrown together. Our differences were real, but they paled before the multiple expressions of faith that swirled around us. We were forced to ask with new urgency; How did we understand the gospel that had sent us, the Christ we served and our mission in bearing witness to him? We searched for common answers with each other in prayer and Bible study. We developed a fellowship that lasted for years, as we dispersed to our various missions in China, and later throughout the world. We also talked with those other missionaries; we argued with them and, where possible, we prayed with them. It was in a way the Church in mission gestating in a ship on the Pacific Ocean. Then one day as we arrived in the port of Shanghai, another world absorbed us.

2. Immersion in China

Immediately, the paradox of China surrounded us. On the one hand, one could feel the vitality of the market, through which we walked from the mission station to the city. Bustle was everywhere. Small merchants sold everything, from food to clothes to machinery, from stalls in front of one story tin-roofed houses in which they lived. Every so often a pedicab would come through, or a human-drawn wagon delivering supplies, but the unpaved street really belonged to the people on foot. It was old China, anchored at one end by a city built by Europeans along the riverfront they called the Bund, and at the other end by a mission school and compound.

On the other hand, China was in chaos. Except in the cities and the south, the national government, the Guomindang, never really established itself after the Japanese invasion which lasted from 1937 to 1945. In 1947 when we arrived in Shanghai the yuan traded at 7,000 to the dollar. Two years later, when the Communists took over the dollar was worth 12 million yen. We had to fly with our baggage from Shanghai to Beijing (in a Lutheran mission plane, the "St. Paul") because the rail lines were cut or continually raided by the Communist guerillas, who roamed, and to a large extent controlled, the countryside. Beijing was a walled city and the walls had meaning. Villages a few miles away had to cope with the government control by day and the Communist control by night. The decay of the Guomindang was evident everywhere; underpaid or unpaid soldiers and police, bribery expected and given at every turn, and a general experience that the government had to be paid off, but was not functional. Students were forbidden to read Communist literature, but, even for Christian students, it was their substance and their inspiration. As one student put it to me, "First we have to have Communism to solve the people's problems. Then we can learn to be Christians." It was a theme that developed in the "Three Self Movement" in years to come. The Communists, in their program of justice for all people and their selfless devotion to the public good, are expressing the love of God. Christians supporting them can deepen the movement and make it more personal by their witness as a church community. So the students and many of their teachers imagined, in Beijing in 1948. They could hardly wait to be, as the jargon went, "liberated."

They were not violent. Ruth was walking home one day with three small children, when a demonstration came down the street. "Down with America and the Guomindang" said the signs, and the shouts of the demonstrator marchers were equally strident. Then one of the students in the crowd came over to her and asked in English, "Would you like to know what we are demonstrating about?" As they walked safely past the militant marchers, he explained their grievances and their hopes.

Meanwhile, the old China was everywhere—in the country villages and in the *hutungs* (narrow streets) between the walled compounds of Beijing. We rented rooms in such a compound with an Australian missionary family, Alec and Jean Yule and their grandchildren. It was part of an old mansion from imperial times with rooms around a plum tree. That was immersion of another kind. We rarely saw our aristocratic landlady. But life in the *hutung* outside the wall bustled with vendors, traders and neighbors dealing with each other. Our cook was negotiating for a wife, and the middleman parked his coal-bearing camels outside our gate.

Then there was Er-Ping. She was a two-year-old, just recovered from scarlet fever, who lived with her mother and two older brothers in a single room in a crowded compound quite different from ours. No plum tree, no garden—just dust. Our missionary colleague Doris Caldwell discovered her (Doris was a joyful combination of social worker and saint). Er-Ping's father had died of tuberculosis. Her mother was sick with it and needed a few weeks' hospitalization. Neighbors in the compound would care for the two older boys, but could we take Er-Ping until her mother came back? We did; one couldn't turn down Doris! On our diet she grew plump and healthy. Then she went back home. Chinese friends explained to Doris that the neighbors were helping the family survive; but if the foreigners did more, they would do less, for all were in need. So life went on, governed by its traditional relations, through poverty, war, invasion and every tribulation.

We were assigned to Cheeloo University in Jina, Shandong, about 250 miles south of Beijing, where I was to be chaplain and instructor in social science. Ruth had spent part of her childhood in a house on the campus where her father was a professor of agriculture there. But the Communists got there first. Jinan was the first major city they occupied outside of Manchuria in North China. The University decided beforehand to move south, in hopes of a few years of peace. There was a precedent. Cheeloo and many other Christian colleges had fled to west China earlier to escape Japanese occupation. So, the Arts and Sciences College of the University, its students, faculty, administration, books, and equipment, took one of the last trains south out of Jinan and settled in rented space in a Buddhist temple outside the city of Hangzhou, southwest of Shanghai. There we joined them.

It was China in another style. The "Temple of the Resting Cloud" (Yun Chi Si) was a ramshackle complex of hundreds of rooms built into the head of a valley that surrounded a central hall presided over by a huge statue of the Buddha. The monks were largely uneducated, but schooled in their life and ceremonies. I remember once when a chanting procession offered prayers at a side altar, ignoring a biology class microscope that was sitting on it. On the whole however, we kept out of each other's way. They only requested that we do not hold Christian public worship inside the temple. So we set up our church in an open shed outside the gate which we were told, had once housed sacrificial animals. Twenty-one students and faculty joined that church after a communicant's class, in early spring. It was my one pastoral success.

For a few months, all was peaceful. By New Year 1949 however, the Communists were already at the Yangtze River, having overrun most of north China. It was clear that they would reach us sometime in the spring. Ruth and I decided that she and our three-year-old son should go to Shanghai, which was a port of exit in case of emergency. We did not fear the Communists. We were concerned, however, about the disorder and destruction that a battle might bring. We need not have worried. Guomindang soldiers and government abandoned the area two weeks before the Communists arrived. The Communists did not conquer China. As in most of the country in 1948-49, they marched into a non-resisting, ungoverned space. But we did not know that then. So, on a February morning we went to a railroad station to catch a train north to Shanghai.

It was bedlam. No one was in the office selling tickets. No one knew about train schedules. Trains went through carrying Nationalist officials to safety in the south. Crowds were everywhere, in the station and on the tracks. We climbed into a train people thought was going north. It wasn't as we found when hours later it began to empty out. We tramped along that platform and met a contingent of Nationalist women soldiers. They were delighted to hear that Ruth had also grown up in Shandong, their home province. "Why are you leaving us?" they asked. It was a poignant question we heard often in those days. They offered to share their rice but we left it to them. Down the tracks we found a train that by consensus was really going to Shanghai. By midnigh when it left, there were sixteen people in our compartment designed for four. Next morning as we detrained, we saw people on the roofs of the cars and hanging from the doors. Chaos but friendly. When our three-year-old had to go, someone would pick him up. Fifteen people passed him over their heads down the corridor to the toilet, then back again to us. That was China in those days.

3. Life under Communism

Ruth and our son left Shanghai just days before it fell, for the Philippines where she worked for a year on the faculty of Silliman University in Dumaguete on the island of Negros where her father was president. I went back to Cheeloo University in the Temple of the Resting Cloud. There we coped with the danger of lawlessness and awaited, in fear and hope for the best, the Communists. Pilgrims streamed to the temple daily by the hundreds, then, all of a sudden in mid-April, they stopped coming. On May 7th, the Eighth Route Army marched by our temple on their way to the city. The students ran down to meet them. There followed three weeks of frenzied efforts to copy the Communist pattern of re-education: the study of Mao Zedong works in the morning followed by criticism and self-criticism—of each other of course, not of Mao. Slogan-shouting followed in the afternoon, and works projects. Then, the students discovered that new authorities in Hangzhou were paying no attention to them. So they went back to school, reinstated their teachers, and finished the semester. Thus we were "liberated."

The University went back to Jinan with all its faculty, students, administration, books and equipment, even including missionaries. There it lasted two years until all Christian colleges in the country were taken over by the government. I was however refused permission to go with them because I had never been to Jinan. Instead I was sent to Shanghai, "the port of exit," the new government pointedly explained.

Shanghai was in peaceful turmoil. On the one hand, all was orderly, to the immense relief of people who had known the uncertainty of decaying government and wild inflation for years. The Communist authorities, government officials and police, were honest to a fault. Corruption disappeared. Foreigners, including missionaries, were free to move about (though not to leave town). People could attend to their business. Churches could worship and Christian bodies could hold meetings as before, and they did. On the other hand, there was, especially in Christian circles, a mood of anxiety somewhat tempered by hope. Kiang Wen-han, general secretary of the Student YMCA, who had oriented me and Ruth to China already in New York, was quietly optimistic. "The Church had a ministry," he said, "to soften with love the hard justice of the Communists." Presiding Bishop Y.Y. Tsu, of the Episcopal Church was more cautious. Y.T. Wu, author of the "Christian Manifesto" later, was ebullient. Under Communist leadership, he could realize the teachings of Jesus. At the National Council of Churches Headquarters, Victor Hayward, a British Baptist missionary with long experience in China, was carefully diplomatic in policy and insightful in his reports. He was a spiritual and political guide, amid all this turmoil, to this young inexperienced missionary. It was he who warned me when I continued by mail from Hong Kong my critical discussion with Kiang Wee-han, that this was putting him in danger.

But the Shanghai sojourn lasted only a few months. I applied, and, by some miracle I was the only missionary granted a permit to go to Nanjing, to replace several missionaries who had left that city. There the mood was optimistic. Under the Guomindang, it had been the capital of the country and the diplomats were still there negotiating with the "People's Government" in Beijing. They included the American Foreign Service along with the Dutch, the British and others. Christian schools, including Nanjing University and Ginling College, operated without hindrance, as did the churches as well. There was hope that life would continue to be normal, that my family could return, and that there might be a future for the Church and even for the missionaries who served it in Communist China.

But we foreigners did not feel the pressure that was intense everywhere else. Groups were organized in every neighborhood, in every factory and shop and in every school to learn new ideology. Mao Zedong's New Democracy was, of course, a standard text. But Marx, Engels and Lenin also appeared, notably in Engels's pamphlet, *From Ape to Man*, which described how humans evolved from apes by learning to use tools in common to master nature. The spirit of it was expressed in a slogan people were taught to shout; "Don't revere heaven …. Don't revere earth. Only revere the power of the people's labor." (It sounds more like a slogan in Chinese!) The study aimed at changing minds and hearts. Participants were pressed to confess their faults: love of self or love of family more than the love of the people. They were pushed to purge themselves not only of imperialistic ideas and loyalty to foreign people or institutions, but also of superstitions, the Party's description of religious belief. This confession was encouraged and driven deeper by criticism from the group and its leader. "Re-education" was the main program of the Communist Party, at least in Nanjing, in the first year of its reign. It seemed as if they were aiming to convert everyone.

Reactions to this re-education among the students—most of whom I knew were Christians—differed. Some were deeply impressed by the idealism and devotion of their Communist teachers. A few were truly converted. "I have become a new man in the classless revolution pioneer corps," wrote one to a missionary friend. "I shall ever live for self, but for the masses." He no longer believed in God, he said, but sent his "revolutionary love." Others were more skeptical. They felt the pressure, both psychological and political, and tried strategies of conforming outwardly while keeping their own counsel within. The Christian Youth Fellowship, most of whom could not answer or resist the pressure, sought in their meetings the assuring presence of the Holy Spirit in exhortation, prayer ad speaking in tongues. These patterns of response persisted over the years, as long as re-education lasted. Whatever their response, they all realized, as some of us foreigners did not, that they were facing a long future of life in Communist society.

There were of course, other Christian and church responses to Communist control as well. In Shanghai 1949, church leaders wrestled with an appropriate Christian response to the revolution that was overwhelming China. The Episcopal Church of China (Sheng Gong Huei), for example, produced a statement which promised support for the revolution but, guided by Christian prophetic understanding rather than a Communist ideology or, at times, Communist practice. But this, and other efforts, were in vain. Within a year it was clear that only the *Communist Manifesto* which combined Christian profession with Communist Party analysis, was acceptable to the government as a basis for the church's official existence. There followed, in ensuing years, staged denunciations in which church leaders publicly denounced missionaries and churchmen who did not conform.

There was the future. But in early 1950, the signs were already there. There was still work for a missionary to do, but I left China then, when it became clear that Ruth and our son Russell would not soon, if ever, be allowed to return. As it turned out, within two years all missionaries were gone from the country, some of them, including friends of mine, after denunciations and public mass trials.

Still, one can only leave China with profound regret, a regret and sadness shared far more deeply by missionaries who had given their lives to China as Ruth and I intended to do. We left many Christian friends there: elders whom I respected and from whom I learned, colleagues with whom I worked, students of whose lives I was a part, including twenty-one whom I confirmed in the church outside the temple in Hangzhou. What became of them? In most cases, I do not know. A few contacts have come, mostly after the collapse of the "Cultural Revolution" in 1976. One, who had denounced me, visited the United States then and shared with me what he had been through in the intervening years, and we were friends again. But for the most part we can only pray for them and see their faces in the new Chinese friends whom we have made. The Chinese are a friendly people. God has made them so. Thank God.

4. Reflections

What then, on a broader scale, have we learned from the Chinese events, that still involves us with that land? I suggest two things.

First, about history: A few years after we left China, in a conference on "The Missionary Church in East and West," the missionary theologian J. Lesslie Newbigin, out of his deep experience in India's traditional culture and social revolution, summed up his perceptions thus:

> The thesis I want to argue is this: that what we are witnessing is the process by which more and more of the human race is being gathered up into that history whose center is the Cross and whose end is the final judgement and mercy of God.[1]

Something like that was happening to China. Traditionally, China's history had looked to the past and to the harmony of heaven and earth, not to the future. The teachings of Confucius and the dynastic chronicles of later times looked backward to a golden age of sage emperors. Confucian metaphysics was static. It expressed the basic harmony of heaven and earth. For 2,000 years, this culture was the basis of the educational system on which political advancement depended. It unified imperial China despite all its wars, famines and social turmoil. Invaders, even if they conquered like the Mongols, were absorbed into it. Religions, such as Buddhism and early Christianity, had their influence but were contained. Foreign trade was managed and controlled through certain ports and roads. It was not central to the economy of the land. China was a self-contained and self-sufficient civilization, the center to which all other peoples were tributary.

Then, beginning in the nineteenth century, this world was attacked from without and, in response, it crumbled within. The first attack, in 1839, was commercial and military. The British, who traded through Guangzhou (Canton), the only port open to foreign ships, were outraged when an imperial officer confiscated a shipment of (illegal) opium. They responded with the "Opium War," sailing up the Yangtze River in central China with gunboats, effectively cutting the country in half. The result was five "treaty ports" (later expanded) where foreigners could not only trade but live under the law of their own countries, exempt from Chinese authority.

The effect on China was not just defeat in war and openness to trade. Over the century that followed, a whole civilization was flooded by the power of Western industry, technology and ideas. The Empire struggled to contain the flood. Its leaders distinguished between body (*ti*) which was the traditional Confucian

---

[1] Charles C. West and David M. Paton, eds., *The Missionary Church in East and West* (London: SCM Press, 1959), 82.

order of China, and the use (*yong*) which was science, technology, economic and military power. They sent students abroad to learn these useful things, hoping to strengthen the body of traditional China. But the use had its own dynamic. It involved China in the history of the rest of the world, and eroded the self-contained body. European (and to some degree, American) industry and finance were more efficient. Western medicine was more effective. Western education and Western politics seemed to equip some people better to cope with the powers that were invading the Chinese world. In 1905, the 2,000-year-old examination system, which had been composed exclusively of the classical Confucian corpus, was abolished. In 1911, the Empire fell, followed by thirty-eight years of domestic and foreign conflict until the Communists unified the nation in 1949. It was also a time of exciting intellectual turmoil. Liberal humanists argued with Marxists about Chinese civilization in revolutionary change. Sun Yat Sen, revered by all as the "Father of Modern China," was a Christian and Western educated leader whose book, *Three Peoples Principles* (San Min Zhu Yi) was a mixture of Christian ethics, Western political philosophies and deep devotion to China, not as a universe but as a nation. Thus, China was drawn into world history.

Christian mission was involved in these events. In one sense, it was part of the Western invasion. Protestant missions spread across China after the Opium War. The Roman Catholic Church emerged from hiding and grew as well. Both used the advantages wrung by Western powers from the Empire for travel, residence, and often personal protection. Mission hospitals practiced Western medicine. Mission schools taught Western science and shed new light on human history both East and West. Christian colleges were centers of Western learning in dialogue with Chinese tradition. My father-in-law, Dr. Arthur Carson, a rural sociologist, worked from one such college, not only to serve the church in its mission, but also, often with Chinese government cooperation, to modernize farming in the Chinese countryside. So it went. Christian missions were among the agents of Western transformation in modern China.

In another sense, however, Christian mission was the vehicle of a message, the gospel Christians call it, of God's judgment on and promise for all the civilizations of the world, including China and all the lands from which missionaries came. It was the message of God's covenant first with Jews, then with all nations in the life, death, resurrection and reign of Jesus Christ now and to come. The Western world had heard this gospel for centuries. It had revolutionized that world more than once, and still confronts it with its judge and savior. Western missionaries brought this gospel very imperfectly to China. In the name of God's love in Christ they did some wonderful things. They liberated family love from Confucian constraints, and educated women for the first time in Chinese history. They created Christian communities held together by faith in the triune God and not by clan or family loyalty. On the other hand, it is easy to describe the theological mistakes they made. Some, especially Roman Catholics, formed enclaves of Christian culture, which they controlled. Some, notably the China Inland Mission, stressed individual conversion and apocalyptic expectation almost to the exclusion of the church. Some Christian scholars tried to synthesize Christian and Confucian views of the divine reality and of human ethics, or at least to minimize the differences between them. Still others identified Christian faith with modernizing China, and drifted toward liberal progressivism or revolutionary Communism. Many foreign missionaries dominated the Christian communities they formed, out of concern for right doctrine, financial responsibility, or efficient management, long after they should have subjected themselves to their Chinese brothers and sisters in the Lord. Despite all this, the message came through. With all their sins, missionaries were still witnesses to the God they served. They planted a church. The church survived, and is struggling to find its own response to God's judgment and promise today.

But we are ahead of the story. Two other gospels, both humanist transformations of the Christian message, won provisional victories. One was enlightenment humanism; the other was Marxist Communism.

Enlightenment humanism led the way. It seemed to coordinate Confucian and Christian traditions around a belief in human goodness and historical progress. It seemed to explain the power and success of modern industry—all with reference to human reason and morality, without the judgment and grace of God. John Dewey and Bertrand Russell made triumphant tours through China with this gospel. Chinese leaders used it to reform the Confucian tradition, to dismantle empire in favor of democracy and the classical language in favor of speech of the people. It introduced Mr. Science, whom one philosopher wrote that China should follow as its new teacher. It was the basis of the technological, industrial and financial forces that destroyed the old structure of Chinese society and plunged it into the global revolution that was changing us all.

But for all that, the gospel of enlightenment humanism failed to rebuild China. Many reasons have been given for this failure. Let me add one more. Enlightenment humanism could appeal to Chinese philosophers, to entrepreneurs and power brokers, both foreign and domestic, who were remolding China, but neither in its Western nor its Chinese version, did it understand the depths of human nature. China, for centuries, was a network of relationships permeated by a sense of harmony of all that is. A foreign scholar whom I read, described with wonder a market town where periodically farmers and craftsmen by the hundreds would bring their wares, set up their stall, bargain with buyers, dismantle and go home again—all without a policeman or an official to be seen. The network was not without cruelty and conflict. It constricted humanity, especially the humanity of women. It defined justice and love in a limited way that undermined the dynamic of both. But it also allowed for escape. Buddhist and Daoist temples provided access to another sphere and other powers, real or imaginary. It was not uncommon for a man who was cheated or wronged beyond endurance to curse the street of his village. Farmers and others pushed by debt or exploitation into extreme poverty often formed bandit gangs or secret societies to prey on others. Several times in history these bandit gangs grew to armies, overthrew the emperor, and established a new dynasty.

All of this, however, could not help the Chinese people cope with the forces that overwhelmed them when they were opened to the rest of the world. Sun Yat Sen tried but did not really understand those forces. Chiang Kai Shek tried to harness the power of Shanghai finance and industry to his vision of the nation. He even worked with Christian missionaries to organize and inspire youth and (with my father-in-law, among others) to modernize education and agriculture. It crumbled under Japanese attack and the corruption of financial power and, after World War II, never recovered. There were stories of Guomindang (Nationalist) generals pocketing the money and not paying the troops. Officials expected bribes for their public services. Government collapsed. During the interregnum after the Guomindang left and the Communists had not yet arrived, I met a nationalist soldier who had taken refuge for the night in our temple on his way south. "Are you American?" he asked. I confessed that I was. "I want to apologize," he said, "for the misuse my government has made of your generous help." We talked a bit, and next day he went on his way. I remember him still.

The humanist ideology that finally conquered China was, of course, Communism. It was totally Western ideology, born of revolt against the inhuman conditions of early capitalism in the European Industrial revolution. Karl Marx was an extreme collective humanist, who believed in the self-creation of humanity by its labor and in the formation of all nature by this labor for human purposes and in the human image. This was paradise or, in his terms, primitive communism. But humanity has fallen, due to the division of labor and private property, which is simply the expropriation of the labor of some by others, thereby depriving them of their true humanity. This process went through slavery, feudalism, and has reached its final stage in the utter inhumanity of wage labor and the accumulation of capital which is, in Marx's words, "congealed labor" used by the few to exploit the many. The consequence is revolution by the exploited masses, the complete reversal of the power structure, and the establishment of a classless society wherein all means of production will be commonly owned and each will contribute freely to the prosperity of all. All this is the law of history, said Marx and Lenin. It will happen, and the Communist Party is the agent of the people to make it so.

What appealed to the Chinese in all this was not the analysis of economic conditions in the West, but the power of revolutionary action to transform the nation. It took the evil of poverty, oppression and inhuman power seriously. It provided a reasoned faith on which people could act with confidence that history was on their side. The powers were different of course. Two thousand two hundred years of Confucian imperial history was dubbed feudalism. The Western incursion, following Lenin's analysis, was labeled capitalistic imperialism, the more so because traders, industrialists and bankers from the West, with some Chinese collaboration, used foreign political and military power to exploit the country.

All these ideas were developed by intellectual leaders. They might have been only theory, but for Mao Zedong. He organized the Party and imbued it with hope and discipline through the years of suffering and combat. His simplified version of Marx and Lenin, laced with expressions from popular Chinese lore, provided its ideology. By 1949 when the communists took over China, there were a million devoted soldiers and a million more political followers who lived by this ideology and this hope. They were incorruptible, dedicated believers. In public offices, they brought order and law to a chaotic society. The currency stabilized. The government was strict but dependable. The whole population, in our area at least, breathed a sigh of relief.

This was, of course, not the end of the story. The first years of Communist control emphasized ideological education. It was an intense effort to change the mind of the whole country. Its aim was conversion. In every village, in every city neighborhood, in every school and factory, small groups were organized under Party leadership. They studied Maoist works, engaged in self- and mutual criticism to root out their imperialist attitudes, their concern for self and family, their private ambitions, their religious "superstitions"—anything that would impede them from wholehearted devotion to the leadership of the People's Government (still the official name of China today). This was followed by purging of "reactionary" elements—village landlords, family leaders, businessmen, scholars and even Christian leaders—who were denounced by friends and colleagues, subjected to mass trials where hundreds hurled accusations against them, sentenced, beaten, and disgraced (and sometimes killed.) Then came the "Great Leap Forward," the collectivization of farms, destruction of ancestral family temples and cemeteries, and the effort to industrialize China by local initiatives, "backyard smelters" and the like. Finally came the Cultural Revolution, the drive to continually purge China and each person of anti-revolutionary habits and attitudes and to exalt physical labor over mental activity as the means for progress. Red Guards roamed the country, encouraged by Mao, destroying vestiges of culture. Schools and universities were closed. Students, teachers, scholars and office workers were sent to work in fields and farms. The results, by common consent, were disastrous. Most Chinese today regard that period as a time of troubles. Many suffered under it.

Deng Xiao Ping, who opened the country to international contacts and private enterprise, is the new father of Chinese policy. The results have been phenomenal. China's economy has grown prodigiously, to the point where it is now, after the United States, the second largest in the world. Relations with the rest of the world have grown. Hundreds of thousands of Chinese have gone abroad for study, and almost as many foreigners are working in China. But there are problems. Air pollution is terrible. Major metropolitan areas are covered with polluted clouds, and China depends on the coal that produces it, for heating and industrial development. On the one hand, cities are growing at a phenomenal rate, but on the other hand, they are smothered in smog. One cannot visit China today without being enveloped by the dilemma. Then there is the question of inequality. The income gap between the city and the countryside increases as the economy grows. Millions of people do not participate in that growth. Furthermore, as private enterprise expands, corruption also increases. Officials are involved along with entrepreneurs. Who guards, and how effectively, the public interest is a major question.

The basic issue underlying all this, however, is this: What has happened to the coherent, disciplined power united by a faith that inspires devotion to a historical destiny? The Communist Party gained this power with such a faith, an ideology which inspired and disciplined millions of followers. That faith, in its excesses, destroyed itself, but the Party is still in total control. Its members are present in every neighborhood, in every school and college, in every factory and bank, everywhere, in short, where people live and decisions are made. It represses dissent, sometimes violently, as on Tiananmen Square in 1989. It imprisons critics. It blocks and manipulates communications. But what does the Party now believe? Marx, Lenin, and Mao are still honored, but their guidance is not sought. There is a move among scholars to revive Confucian ethics as a moral basis for society. But China has been swept into history; it is no longer the self-contained universe of the Confucian worldview. On what basis can these rulers control modern technological, financial and military power to achieve their ends, and what ends do they want to achieve? The field is wide open.

This leads to my second reflection: the witness of the Christian church to the judgment and promise of God. The story of Christianity in the last sixty years is remarkable. At first, the Communist attack was standard Leninist. It was directed first of all against Christian faith, as in the West. One of the pamphlets in the re-education program was Friedrich Engels's *From Ape to Man* which taught that human beings created themselves by learning to use tools. The picture was of an ape under a tree on which hung, out of reach, a piece of fruit. When the ape learned to use a stick to reach the fruit, that was the beginning of its development toward becoming. A human being, not God, created humanity. But divine creation was never a Confucian, Buddhist or Taoist belief. The Communists were reacting to a Judeo-Christian understanding of history. They were proclaiming collective humanity as masters of that history, not the God who chose the Jews and came on earth as Jesus Christ. That was the same history, into which China had been brought. The question was, who is its lord, and what is its destiny?

The Communists tolerated religion, carefully controlled to support and not hinder the progress of the revolution, until this false comfort was no longer needed. So the "Three-Self Movement," self-governance, self-support and self-propagation, was organized for Protestants to free them from foreign influence, and the "Patriot Church for Catholics" to free them from papal control. To this day, only churches registered with these organizations are recognized by the government.

There were about 700,000 Protestant believers in China in 1949. They were harassed continually, and almost driven underground during the Cultural Revolution. Yet today, official figures count eighteen million registered Protestants, and this only begins to tell the story. The figure is an arbitrary convention, which serves the Christians to conceal their growth, and the government to belittle their problem. The actual number of Christians, many in unregistered churches, is unknown. I have heard one estimate (by a Chinese sociologist) of 130 million. Most estimates run somewhat less, but still several times the official count.

In addition, there are many "cultural Christians" among the intellectuals, who knew Christian history and count themselves adherents, though they were not members of churches. In university philosophy and religion departments which I have visited since 1996, Marxism is taught but is not influential. There are attempts to revive Buddhism and Taoism. But the main interplay is between the attempt to modernize Confucianism, with help from Western thought, and Christian theology. One encounter dramatizes this interplay. It happened at a dinner hosted by the dean of a provincial university. He must have been a Communist Party member, but he presented an earnest reflection on Confucianism as the future moral basis of Chinese society. I asked another faculty member for his input. "No," he said, "The question is not what reason dictates, but whom do you trust?" He then explained that Christ was the one he trusted, and he built his philosophy in relation to that reality. The dean did not dispute his colleague. That was in itself remarkable. But more remarkable was the insight it gave into what goes on in academic areas where the meaning of life and society is a serious question.

All these Christians face an enormous opportunity and challenge as they look to the future. Enlightenment and Communist humanism were powerful in bringing China into history. They failed because they misjudged human nature and therefore rejected or misread the coming of Jesus Christ in that history. They turned God's covenant, judgment and promise into a human operation. But God is still at work, and the Christ whom we crucified has risen and points the way to a world more human and more hopeful. China is open for witness to this humanity and to its hope.

III.   EUROPE AND THE *OIKOUMENE*

1. Why?

In June 1950, Ruth and son Russell joined me in Hong Kong. They came by boat from Dumaguete in the southern Philippines, where she had spent a busy year working with friends at Silliman University where also her father was president and she had spent two happy years at high school before the war. I came by coastal ship from China.

Now what are we to do? Everywhere the world was rebuilding after a devastating war. Revolution was in the air all over the world, not only in China. Basic questions of faith, culture, and social change were being raised in Asia, Africa, Latin America and Europe. Only North America, Australia and the Pacific Islands seemed to be spared the intensity of it. Nationalist, Communist and other ideologies were in competition everywhere, and Christian mission was in the midst of it all. China was closed, but we could have gone anywhere else and joined the fray. Ruth would have been happy to take me back to the Philippines and to Silliman University in a newly independent country. I would gladly have stayed in Hong Kong, joining the growing company of Christian workers, Protestant and Catholic, who were trying to understand events in China, interpret them in the church and to the world, hoping that one day they might return to that country. But it was not to be. The Presbyterian Board of Foreign Missions did not think it wise at the time to support workers whose primary job was to interpret and observe.

That brought Europe into view. Why? It might seem strange that American missionaries should serve there. It was, after all, the cradle of Christian civilization, in which many of the churches in other continents, including the United States, had been born and nourished. Why were we called to go half way around the world to continue our mission in the continent of our ancestors? Well, as we look back there were reasons for that call.

First, the whole vision of the Church of Jesus Christ in mission had changed. In the nineteenth century, missionaries had gone out from churches in Europe and the United States, where Christianity was dominant for centuries, with the Christian message for other lands. They gathered believers and formed new churches in every part of the world. China's experience was happening in Africa, Asia, the Pacific Islands and everywhere. But these new churches were also missional, not to their own cultures, but also to us who had been Christians for centuries. How does Christ judge and transform Western culture, power, science, technology and money which accompanied those missionaries, and which the rest of the world has experienced as imperialism? What is the Christian witness to nationalism; not only in its extreme Nazi and Fascist forms that had both challenged and subverted European churches, but also in the national pride we carry with us, to whatever nation we belong? What is our gospel to exploited, alienated people who found in Marxist movements their strategy and their hope, not only in China and India but in Europe as well? These were worldwide questions, and they still are, differently mixed with different cultures, but facing us all.

The mission of Christ's church is one in the whole world, to discern and make known the judging and redeeming ways of God in every society and in the life these societies live together. It is the calling of all Christians everywhere. What is more appropriate than that we, American missionaries, should try to serve that mission as emissaries between China and Europe?

Second, Europe itself was devastated by the Second World War. Churches in the USA reached out together to churches in that devastated continent. They called it "the sharing of ecumenical resources." Material relief was an important part of it, of course. Human need was basic, for food, for clothing, for rebuilding destroyed buildings and communities. But the spirit was not one of giving and receiving. We needed to learn from them what it means to follow Christ in the midst of resistance and war. We were part of a common mission, "partners in obedience" as one ecumenical conference phrased it, in which all the resources of the church, material and spiritual, were involved. If American churches had more material resources, including the ability to move people around, those resources belonged to God and should be shared. So, with Ruth's support I wrote to Charles Arbuthnot, an admired friend who was the Presbyterian Church's representative in Europe. Could I, with my study of ethics and Communism and my experience in China, be of some use there?

The answer was immediate. Come! We would be "fraternal workers," as Charles and Genis Arbuthnot had been when they served with the Reformed Church of France immediately after the war. We would be assigned by our church to an agency of the church in Germany—it turned out to be the Gossner mission to industrial workers—to be a friend, a helper, and a representative of ecumenical fellowship as the church was rebuilding after the war. Thus began the second phase of our ministry.

2. Geneva and the Ecumenical Movement

But first we flew to Geneva, to the headquarters of the World Council of Churches. That was the third reason for wanting to serve in Europe. Spiritually, Geneva was like Rome is to the Roman Catholic, but much less wealthy and formal. I had become a Christian inspired by the witness of Robert Mackie and the World Student Christian Federation (WSCF). Its headquarters were part of a modest building in Rue Calvin in the old city of Geneva. The World Council of Churches had celebrated its inauguration two years before in Amsterdam, one of the great events of the twentieth century. Visser't Hooft, whose book had convinced me of the Christian faith, was its general secretary. Robert Mackie became director of Interchurch Aid and Service to Refugees. The Council operated them out of a chalet on Geneva's Route de Malagnou, with barracks and buildings alongside it where denominational associations and member churches had their offices, including Charles Arbuthnot and the Presbyterian Church U.S.A.

The world was there. I learned that thousands had shared my experience and been inspired by the ecumenical vision of unity in Christ and serving Christ's mission to the world. The staff of the World Council of Churches was drawn from them. Every day in common worship, in offices, or at the 4 p.m. tea where everyone broke and mingled, one could not only meet French, Dutch Germans, Danes, Norwegians, Swedes and Finns along with a few British and North Americans, an occasional Swiss (we were, after all, in Switzerland), but also Indians and other Asians, Africans and Eastern Orthodox. They were experiencing, many for the first time, what the Communion of the Holy Spirit means. They were planning for an ecumenical future: one God in Christ for the world.

Who were these people? In the cloud of witnesses, one cannot do justice to them all. With a prayer for forgiveness for those I have missed (I shall meet them all in the Communion of Saints one day), let me say a word about some who stand out in my memory.

Visser 't Hoof, the Dutchman who found his faith, as I did later, in the Student Christian Movement. He had spent years as general secretary of the WSCF, when he wrote *None Other Gods* which played such a role in my conversion but when I met him, he was general secretary of the World Council of Churches which he had helped to form. More about him later when I was on his team. Here let me only state that in my view, he was one of the great men of the twentieth century. His always relevant theological insight, his firm yet open leadership, his faith-based ecclesiological diplomacy, built the World Council of Churches as an institution which was also a movement. He brought together the churches of the world in prayer, evangelism and prophecy, always staking the future on faithfulness to the judgment, promise and mercy of God. In all of this he was a colleague and a friend as well. This is how I met him at the old, informal headquarters at the Route de Malagnou, and knew him later as a member of his team. Robert Mackie was the same tough ecumenical Christian. He had to be to run his department! But he was also more accessible. He gathered a group of us young folk one evening to explore our thoughts as he had done for years in traveling for the WSCF. He helped make us a community. Ten years later I had the privilege of contributing to editing with him a book, *The Sufficiency of God in Honor of Visser 't Hooft*. He not only brought me, as a college student, through the WSCF into the Christian church. He was also an elder friend, teacher and colleague in that faith.

Out at the Ecumenical Institute in the Chateau de Bossey, twelve miles up the lake from Geneva, were two other ecumenical leaders, Hendrik Kraemer and Suzanne de Dietrich. We had no idea when we visited them that summer that we would be among their successors on the Bossey staff. But we knew we were in the presence of elders in the faith and in the church.

Suzanne de Dietrich had been Visser 't Hooft's and later, Mackie's colleague in the World Student Christian Federation. She was

French, she was lay, she walked with two canes from her physical disability, and she was an inspiring teacher. She took the scholarship of the biblical renewal that was sweeping Europe between the wars and made the Bible live for a whole generation of students in the Student Christian Movement. Many of our colleagues in the World Council of Churches had known and learned from her. I still have notes on her biblical expositions of peace, justice and freedom given to East German lay people in Berlin.

Hendrik Kraemer was already an established scholar and church leader when he came to Bossey. In his youth he was in Indonesia and profoundly influenced the Christian movement there, "From Mission Field to Independent Church in an Islamic Country," to use the title of his reflections on that experience. In midlife, he was professor of the History of Religion at the University of Leiden. In 1936, he was asked to write on the theology of mission for the International Missionary Conference in Tambaram, India. Two years later his book, *The Christian Message in a Non-Christian World*, was a blockbuster. His basic thesis was that biblical realism, the revelation of the judgment and grace of God in Christ, drives Christian mission; and that human religions and cultures, including Christian religion and culture, are subject to that judgment and can be transformed by that grace. His argument encouraged many, and offended others who were reaching for a synthesis of religious aspirations. He was a pole of controversy on the world stage. Then came World War II. Kraemer became a spiritual leader of Dutch resistance to the Nazi occupation of the Netherlands. "Dutch Reformed Church," he was quoted as saying, "Do you know what it means to be the Church of Jesus Christ?" It was a mission in faith and action, to his own people. Post-war, he was asked to complete his career as founder and director of an Ecumenical Institute whose mission was to bring together Christians from everywhere, lay and ordained, to consider their faith and witness, among the ruins of a world destroyed. We didn't know it then, but we were meeting the man who founded the enterprise Ruth and I were to join six years later.

Here, I must introduce one other great leader whose mantle I was also privileged to touch in those years. He is Joseph Houldsworth Oldham, Joe to his friends, though I could never call him that. He was living in retirement in Sussex, England, not in Geneva, but his influence was everywhere. In a long life he had been a missionary in India, a mission educator for the Church of Scotland; the organizing secretary of the first World Mission Conference in Edinburgh 1910; a founder and first general secretary of the International Missionary Council and founding editor of its journal, the *International Review of Mission,* which is still published today; organizer of the World Conference on Church, Community and State in Oxford 1937, whose seven volumes I studied in seminary; and one of the architects of the World Council of Churches at its inaugural Assembly in Amsterdam 1948. But mission was his lifelong passion. *Faith on the Frontier,* the title of Keith Clements' authoritative biography, catches his spirit well. During the war, he had gathered a group of scholars to explore the frontiers of their disciplines and of national policy in relation to Christian faith. In 1952 he moved to Dunford in Sussex, England but, ever the missionary, he invited groups of younger people to weekends in his home.

This is how I got involved. Ronald Gregor Smith, editor of the Student Christian Movement (SCM) Press, sent him my reflections on China, later published as *Christian Witness in Communist China* under the pseudonym "Barnabas." I had learned from Victor Hayward among others, how not to get Chinese friends in trouble. Oldham liked them. Not only that, he invited me to two of his weekends, where the discussion ranged across physics, sociology, politics, chemistry, philosophy and theology, all with the missionary question in mind, how does one understand these fields in faith? Thus began a correspondence that lasted into the time when I worked at the Ecumenical Institute. Indeed, he prepared me for that ministry. He introduced me to the writings of Karl Popper, Michael Polanyi and Karl Mannheim among others. He led me, fifty years his junior, to understand the mission of the church as an intellectual as well as a practical frontier.

There were also younger workers in Geneva, just a few years older than I, who had caught the ecumenical vision and were putting it into practice. Bob (Robert S.) Bilheimer was director of Studies. He had made his name as Visser't Hooft's right hand man in organizing the Amsterdam Assembly and was now coordinating the fields of study—Faith and Order, Evangelism, Mission, and Church and Society, to which he added Church and the Race Problem—which brought the churches' diverse streams of theology and practice into dialogue and common witness. He served until

1962, then returned to the United States where he found his calling again as director of the Institute for Ecumenical and Cultural Research in Collegeville, Minnesota. Wolfgang Schweitzer, his colleague in Biblical Studies, came out of the last days of the Confessing Church struggle in Germany. He went on later to teach Christian Ethics in Bethel, the seminary founded by Freidrich von Bodelsschwingh in connection with his Center for Ministry to the Disabled. His wife taught us German and we learned from them both a great deal about German life and culture.

IV.   MY ECUMENICAL FRIENDS

There were others: Erik Nielsen of the Department of Mission Studies, who later translated my Barnabas book on China into Danish; Charles Arbuthnot our Presbyterian supervisor, who was a model to us all of principled yet genial ecumenical diplomacy; Stephen Neill, the WCC Associate General Secretary and brilliant historian of mission; Johannes C. (Hans) Hoekendijk, the radical critic of church institutions in the name of the gospel; and many more. But I would like to highlight two who were lifelong friends and working companions.

One of them was **Paul Abrecht**. I had known him briefly in Union Theological Seminary when we were preparing to go to China, and he, with his wife Audrey to the World Council of Churches in Geneva. He was, from 1948 until he retired in 1984, the Director of the Church and Society Office in the World Council of Churches. I was drawn into the work on Church and Society, and stayed with it as long as Paul Abrecht was its leader. It was one of the streams that flowed into the World Council of Churches. The others were the Faith and Order Movement which sought the unity we have in Christ in the face of our divisions of doctrine and order, and Mission, out of whose calling to one gospel for the world the whole ecumenical movement rose. They each had their areas of study and their conferences, but they intermingled in the intimacy of the Malagnou headquarters in those early days. This was the context in which Paul Abrecht worked. But to understand the significance of his ministry requires a bit of history.

M. M. Thomas:

Madathilparampil Mammen Thomas, "M.M." to everyone who knew him, was Indian, a youth leader in the Mar Thoma Church, and politically a radical. I understand that in his youth he applied for ordination in his church and was turned down because of his politics. Then he applied for membership in the Communist Party and was rejected because he was a believing Christian. The first time I met M.M. Thomas was in Geneva, Switzerland in 1950. He was Asian Secretary of the World Student Christian Federation (WSCF) at the time. Paul Abrecht, the Study Secretary of the World Council of Churches (WCC) for Church and Society told me I must meet him. But where was he? I remember the conversation in Abrecht's office: "Oh you can't reach him now. He's off somewhere meditating. He'll turn up eventually." He did, and I met him.

The last time I saw M.M. was when Ruth and I spent a night at his brother's house in Ernakulam. He had entertained us at his home in Tiruvalla and given us a boat tour of the inner passage in Kerala, and was to send us on a tour of Cochin in the morning. At daybreak, however, we heard the tones of the Mar Thoma liturgy. He and his brother were praying it.

That was M.M.; the foundation of his life. I could rejoice in it, argue with its theology, exchange insights with it, but I could never penetrate its depths. To do so would require being steeped in Mar Thoma piety, the Malayalam language, and the experience of India. But we were part of an ecumenical movement seeking the Church's witness to God's promise for the world. So began a life-long friendship.

It began with a letter I wrote him about an article he had written with Malcolm Adiseshiah in the 1947 *Student World*. I, a young missionary in China, thought they described Christian participation in the world revolution in too Marxist terms. It was probably the difference between the Indian experience and mine in China.

In any case, I misjudged the man. In the next issue he described his experience in the World Christian Youth Conference in Oslo, 1947. Indonesian students were there but they refused to take part unless the Dutch, with whom they were at war, were excluded. The meeting was in danger of collapse when Visser't Hooft rose to express, on behalf of the whole Dutch delegation, their repentance for their country's imperial domination. The Dutch and the Indonesians talked all night and declared next morning that they all were in need of the judgment and the forgiving grace of God as they worked together in the hope of the risen and coming Christ's promises for the world.

M.M. took this experience to the World Federation of Democratic Youth in Prague. Here there was no repentance, no reconciliation. There were only friends and enemies, and the call to revolutionary action. Christians are unreliable partners against oppression, they said, with their self-criticism and their talk about forgiveness and grace. That, said M.M., is the witness Christians have to bear. It is weakness, to revolutionaries and also to status-quo self-righteous. It is the strength of the Church in a revolutionary age. All this inspired me before I even met him! Later, he developed this theme in a WSCF book with Davis McCaughey: *The Christian in the World Struggle*. It is a book that has guided my thought ever since.

M.M. went back to India where for the next thirty years, as Director of the Christian Institute for the Study of Religion and Society, he produced a library of books on Christian faith and Indian society, some written by himself, some group efforts by Indian Christians, which he gathered and edited. I, at his invitation, had a modest part in this enterprise, defining the secular as a Christian understanding, over against a Hindu view of religion and society. Later we were colleagues, as consultants to the "Working Committee on Church and Society of the World Council of Churches," and wrote many reports together. He sent students later to study at Princeton Seminary and even came himself as visiting professor. M.M. Thomas was a friend and teacher his whole life. I felt I knew India through him.

Though M.M. went back to India, he did not surrender his ecumenical ties. I worked with him in the Church and Society Working Committee of the WCC for years, and admired his crowning achievement in this field in the management of the World Conference on Church and Society in Geneva in 1966. It was no wonder that he was elected Chair of the Central Committee of the WCC from 1968 to 1975. He showed his understanding of the Faith and Order and the Mission dimensions of the ecumenical movement in his reports and recommendations to the Committee during those years.

But his heart was in India. The first engagement when he returned there was political. He admired Nehru but he did not join the Congress Party. He preferred to prod it from the left by supporting not the Communists but the Socialist Party. But his main concern was Nehru's secularism, which was the basis of his politics. Thomas, in an article in *Religion and Society*, is grateful for the tolerance, the openness and the sense of history (what he calls the Semitic strain) of Nehru's secularism but finds his humanistic view of the human less satisfying. So, a Christian can be grateful that

Nehru has established a secular democratic state without sharing the secularist faith that Nehru brought to it.

This issue of *Religion and Society*, under M.M.'s editorship, was broader than Nehru. It dealt with "secularism and India today." It included my essay on the origin of secularism in the Semitic understanding of history and the distinction between secularism as an optimistic humanism and the secular mood of Western culture today. It included a contribution from P.D. Devanandan on *sarvodaya* as a secularizing tradition in Hinduism and by a sociologist Ram Singh on the challenge to Indian culture of secular science, among others. The message, according to Thomas in his editorial, is that we as Christians should welcome the secularizing tendencies in both politics and culture because it "has made possible for the Church to recover the essential nature of the gospel namely, that Jesus Christ transcends all cultures and is the word of God for their judgment and renewal."[1]

This led to Christian ethics for India to which, alongside his ecumenical activities, M.M. devoted his life until retirement, as Director of the Christian Institute for the Study of Religion and Society (CISRS). In the 1960s and '70s under M.M.'s leadership, research teams worked leading to the publication of several path breaking books that redefined religion and ethics in the Indian context. I used the library he had produced to introduce my students to social ethics in its ecumenical dimension. Later he sent his colleagues in CISRS to study at Princeton Seminary, notably E.V. Mathew, a lawyer whose children are still my good friends, Saral Chatterjee, his successor, and K.C. Abraham, later director of Doctoral Studies for the Serampore system (in Bangalore), who earned his PhD at Princeton Seminary. M.M. was even himself invited by the faculty and came to Princeton for two years as guest professor of World Christianity. I tried to reciprocate with three visits to Bangalore and Kerala, giving support to his ecumenical leadership.

The young M.M. Thomas among them, repeatedly brought home to Westerners the exhilaration and challenge of societies emerging from colonialism and going through in two generations, the multiple revolutions that had taken Europe four centuries. The question was how these revolutions are to be understood in the purpose of God.

---

[1] *Religion and Society*, IX no. 1 (1962), 3.

V.   OXFORD CONFERENCE

"Church and Society" grew out of the Universal Christian Conference on Life and Work, which held its first assembly in Stockholm in 1925. It was the first meeting of divided churches in centuries, devoted to Christian social service and witness. But it was only the opening scene of an ecumenical drama that still continues. The next was the "Conference on Church, Community and State," organized by Oldham, in Oxford 1937.

There the whole tone was different. There had been a world-wide depression. The economic structure of the capitalist world had collapsed. Fascist dictators had strengthened their grip on Germany, Italy, and later Austria and Spain. Japan had conquered part of China and was at war with the rest of it. The League of Nations had failed to curb Japanese aggression in Manchuria, Nazi rearmament of the Rhineland, or, finally, Italian conquest of Ethiopia. That was the end of its political peacemaking force. The world lived in powerless fear of fascist aggression, and of war which finally came despite all attempts at compromise.

Meanwhile revolution was in the air, in every country. Marxism was its most consistent ideology, but Jewish, Christian and pragmatic humanist ideas were in it as well. The question was: What could empower the people of the world to resist the catastrophic control of moneyed power and establish justice (a Hebrew-Christian word) in society? Extreme in their answer were the Communists. "Support and follow the Soviet Union." They were strongest in France, Italy, Spain, and in Germany before the Nazis. Others, Marxist, Christian and other socialists, resisted the Communists, rejected their strong-arm methods, and worked for more democratic change. But all were convinced that revolution in some form must come.

The churches also changed. Already in the 1920s, religion, especially the Orthodox Church, was being systematically repressed in the Soviet Union and the Orthodox emigrès in France and the US were struggling to cope spiritually with the situation. Karl Barth, the theological giant of the twentieth century, proclaimed the word of God in the same decade, over against the Culture-Christianity of Europe. In Germany the issue came to a head when Hitler appointed his own bishop in Berlin who forbade the ordination of pastors who were Jewish by race. The Church split. The Confessing Church issued the Barmen Declaration (largely composed by Barth), created its own organization, claimed to be the Church of Jesus Christ in Germany, and fought the Nazi church leadership till the end of Hitler's regime. Nor were other churches spared. The leading Anglican of his time, William Temple, the Archbishop of York and later of Canterbury, gave theological depth to socialism. In the United States, and throughout the English speaking world, Reinhold Niebuhr brought many into Christian faith with his theology of God's judgment and grace, and his radical politics. The World Student Christian Association, under the leadership of Visser 't Hooft and Suzanne de Dietrich, led a biblical rediscovery of the living word of God in encounter with other worldviews among students world-wide. All these influences spread among the churches. Everywhere the ideological conflict raged, and Christians were in the middle of it.

It was a challenged, repentant, but profoundly hopeful body of Christians that met at Oxford in 1937. The way was prepared by forty-six authors, leaders in theology and social thought from their various churches and disciplines, writing in seven volumes which were studied by theological students (like me) the world over during the next decade. The conference itself drew delegates from forty countries and a wide spread of confessions from Old Catholic to Eastern Orthodox to Reformed, to Methodist, to Lutheran to Baptist, to united churches and others as well. They were seeking the form of their unity in Christ in a common witness to the world. The spirit of the meeting was eloquently expressed in the first paragraphs of the message, sent by all the participants to the churches from which they came. I take the liberty of quoting them here at length because they express so well the spirit of the whole ecumenical movement of which I was a part. (I have modernized the language.)

A MESSAGE FROM THE OXFORD CONFERENCE TO THE CHRISTIAN CHURCHES

"In the name of Christ, greetings."

"We meet at a time when humankind is oppressed with perplexity and fear. Men and women are burdened with evils almost insupportable and with problems apparently insoluble. Even in countries which are at peace, unemployment and malnutrition sap people's strength of body, mind and spirit. In other countries war does its 'devil's work' and threatens to overwhelm us all in its limitless catastrophe."

"Yet we do not take up our task as bewildered citizens of our several nations, asking if anywhere there is a clue to our problems; we take it up as Christians, to whom is committed 'the word of reconciliation that 'God was in Christ reconciling the world unto himself.'"

"The first duty of the church, and its greatest service to the world, is that it be in very deed the church—confessing the true faith, committed to the fulfillment of the will of Christ, its only true Lord, and united in him in a fellowship of love and service."

"We do not call the world to be like ourselves, for we are already too like the world. Only as we ourselves repent, both as individuals and as corporate bodies, can the church call others to repentance. The call to ourselves and to the world is to Christ."

In this faith and with this spirit, they analyzed the ideological struggles and political conflicts of their world and developed ecumenical Christian guidance that provided a context for their churches' community and witness through the years of war to come. In the same year, 1937, these churches formed the World Council of Churches in Process of Formation, named Visser 't Hooft as provisional general secretary, and set 1941 as the year of formal inauguration.

Then World War II intervened. Visser 't Hooft was confined to Geneva, where he became a channel of communication among the churches on both sides of the conflict and with the rest of the world as well. He was in living contact with the German Confessing Church, with the Dutch, French and other churches in resistance to the Nazis, as well as with churches in the United States and Asia who could visit him in that officially neutral city. Robert

Mackie did the same for the World Student Christian Federation until, with his family, he escaped across Vichy France to neutral Portugal, and thence travelled the world visiting every Student Christian Movement he could, including the Christian Association at Columbia where I first met him. He recorded it all in *The Student World* which he edited, an inspiring journal that brought thousands, including me into the world-wide Christian fellowship. It all strengthened the Ecumenical Movement. The churches shared their suffering and their resistance, but most of all they learned to trust one another with the depth that can only come from recognizing in each other the Spirit of God at work in Christ. They were ready, in the summer of 1948 in Amsterdam, to form the World Council of Churches.

It was a magnificent occasion. 351 delegates from 147 churches in 44 countries, in every continent and island where there are Christian people, gathered in that city. The visitors numbered in the thousands. The theme was "Man's Disorder and God's Design." The subthemes, each introduced, as they were at Oxford, by a book with contributions from various churches and countries, were:

    1. The Universal Church in God's Design;

    2. The Church's Witness to Design;

    3. The Church and the Disorder of Society; and

    4. The Church and the International Disorder.

All were substantive, but I shall concentrate on section 3, which wove the Life and Work Movement into the WCC's program.

Many great minds of the church introduced the subject: Searle Bates writing from China; M.M. Thomas from India; Jacques Ellul from France; Kathleen Bliss from Britain; John Bennett, my teacher from Union Theological Seminary, who argued with Constantine Patijn, an economist from the Netherlands, about middle axioms to guide the Christian ethical life; and Reinhold Niebuhr who reminded the Assembly that God's love in Christ is the final judgment and redemption of human failure to end conflict and achieve justice, and that therefore the forgiveness of sins is the basis of all human politics. But it was J.H. Oldham, the veteran of the Ecumenical Movement, who pointed the way for Christian service and witness in the post-war world.

First, he described the dynamics of a world exploding with the achievements and vision of science and technology and at the same time dominated by confidence in human capacity as "explorer, conqueror and architect" to "run the world in accordance with their own ideas" without the need for God. But then, he pointed out, two things have happened: first, "in the process of gaining control over physical nature, [people] have called into existence a vast network of forces and intricate organization, which they are not able, effectively to control"; and second, this control "lays on [them] a terrifying and well-nigh intolerable responsibility of choice," "Without support, without security of any kind, man has to decide at every moment what man is going to be." (In those days, "man" was used generically to mean "human.")

But this individual control of things is the way to nothingness. Men and women become human "in the living give-and-take, the mutual obligation and responsibility of a society of persons," in response to God. This is the calling of the Church. It is only in God's grace and truth that human communities of love and creative service can grow. The Church therefore should be this community in its worship and life. It is also concerned that society be built on "direct and responsible relations" of persons with other persons.

This, said Oldham, is responsible society. It was defined in the Section III report as "one where freedom is the freedom of men who acknowledge responsibility to justice and public order, and where those who hold political authority or economic power are responsible to God and the people whose welfare is affected by it." It is not a system, a structure, or an ideology. It is rather a way of ordering power to just social ends which are always being redefined in free and respectful discernment of the judgment and promise of God in human relations. On this basis, both Oldham and the Section III report criticized the then dominant ideologies and practices of both Marxist Communism and laissez-faire capitalism, and projected a new Christian way of bearing witness in society.

All of this Paul Abrecht inherited when he joined the World Council of Churches staff in 1949. It was like a new orchestra with a new conductor. The overture had sounded. The themes were clear. The enthusiasm of the players was great, though some of them, notably Oldham, had retired. But there was a world of revolutionary change out there to be explored. Science, technology and business were transforming society. Western empires were dismantling. Other societies than Euro-American, in which the Church was also rooted, were awakening to their role in global history. In the thirty-four years of his tenure, Paul Abrecht led the churches into all of this as a great conductor would. He expanded the ecumenical repertoire with ideas and social witness from all parts of the world and from every discipline of the common life. He recruited new players from every continent who brought their experience and their perspective to the dialogue. He did the same for economists, businessmen, and scientists as well, whether they were church members or not. And he did it all from a Church and Society office that often consisted only of him and a secretary, and never included more than five colleagues plus a few volunteers like me.

Paul was an explorer of the vast ecumenical domain. He developed a style and a faith which still characterizes ecumenical activity at its best. The style came from Oldham. One gathers the best minds who are willing to help the churches understand and bear responsible witness to the world in its various dimensions. Then one distributes the results of their deliberations to the churches for action and correction. This leads to further dialogue, to more understanding and truer guidance for the churches' service and witness.

The faith goes deeper, and has permeated the whole Ecumenical Movement. It was typified by a remark Visser 't Hooft made in a Church and Society session where passions ran high and agreement seemed impossible: "It is critical that we not decide that we shall succeed." The Ecumenical Movement from the beginning was a venture of faith. The World Council of Churches as an institution or any of its meetings might not succeed. Success was not its object; faithful witness to the will and promise of God was. That meant profound struggle between those with different views of what, in social policy, that witness should be. But it was a struggle in the presence of God, hoping that God's judgment on human opinions and God's forgiveness of human bias would open the way to new truths.

This style, this faith and this hope was Paul Abrecht's. M.M. Thomas called it evangelical witness to society, with reason. The first office-sponsored conference was with the East Asian Christian Conference in Lucknow, India in 1952. Then followed the Church and Society section of the Second Assembly of the World Council of Churches in Evanston, Illinois in 1954, where churches from the European-American West, the Communist East (Protestant churches from Hungary, Czechoslovakia and East Germany) and the Global South comprising of Asia, Africa and Latin America wrestled with each other to define Christian responsibility in common and for their particular areas. The report came in three sections. The Global South section was largely adoption by the whole Assembly of the Lucknow findings. The section on church witness in Communist society took the form of both sides raising questions to the witness of the other. The third section dealt with all the problems of social justice in democratic societies. One of its achievements was to transcend the concepts, "socialism" and "capitalism," and ask concretely what should be the role of government in the common interest, and what should be the place of the market and private initiative in a responsible society.

After Evanston, several things happened. First, stimulated by M.M. Thomas and others, the Church and Society office plunged into a study of "Christian Responsibility toward Areas of Rapid Social Change." Projects were started and conferences were held in Asia, Africa and Latin America, culminating in a world conference in Thessaloniki, Greece in 1959. Its report was titled *Dilemmas and Opportunities* and its content reflects insights in both dimensions.

Second, under the leadership of Pope John XXIII and the Second Vatican Council, the latent desire of Roman Catholic believers to participate in the ecumenical movement was released and flowered. In social witness this took the form of SODEPAX, an initiative on Society, Development and Peace, sponsored jointly by the Church and Society Department (Paul Abrecht) of the World Council of Churches and the Commission on Justice and Peace of the Roman Catholic Church. For a few years, Protestant, Catholic and Orthodox worked together to focus Christian responsible witness in world society. The SODEPAX reports are still worth reading in this regard.

Third, in 1961 at the Third Assembly in New Delhi, churches in Soviet dominated areas joined the World Council of Churches. The way had long been prepared by visits and negotiations, and it changed the face of the Council. Previously the only member churches from Eastern Europe had been Protestant, from East Germany, Czechoslovakia and Hungary. Now the Orthodox, led by the Russian Orthodox Church, joined in the force. Politics was involved of course. The Russians and others were limited in what they could say. On the other hand, foreign Christians who visited could speak freely, and East Europeans were happy and grateful.

They could use these contacts to enlarge space for the church and its message in their countries. So, a mutual understanding grew as relationships developed.

Fourth, was the explosive event of the World Conference on Church and Society in 1966, with the theme, "Christians in the Technical and Social Revolutions of Our Time." It was designed to be another Oxford Conference but speaking with a world voice to the world of its time. Four books with chapters by Christians from every continent were published in preparation (Full disclosure: my chapter on "Community, Christian and Secular" in M.M. Thomas ed., *Man in Community*, was one of them.) For the first time lay people, not clergy, were in the majority. Roman Catholics, liberated by Vatican II, were there. So were the Orthodox from the East. But the greatest conflict was between what I described in my book, *The Power to be Human*, as the technologists and the revolutionaries. Both were committed to just social change. But the technologists were thinking in terms of economic development and trade policy; the revolutionaries in terms of political power. They were suspicious of each other. The revolutionaries repudiated "responsible society" as a way of thinking about social policy that confirmed the Global North in its security and dominance. The responsible society advocates regarded the revolutionaries as irrational protesters who did not face reality. The reports of the conference did not reflect this tension, but it was there. It was expressed in discussion of the relation of ideology to social analysis and the justification of violence in the struggle for justice. It was also expressed in further policies of the World Council of Churches, the Program to Combat Racism and the Christian Commission to Promote Development, which engaged the Council in social conflict.

All of this was a challenge to Paul Abrecht, who had built his work on bringing Christians of different perspectives together to subject their biases to mutual correction and to the word of God. But he was undismayed. He threw himself into what may have been his crowning achievement, a ten-year study of Faith, Science and the Future culminating in a world conference whose reports, *Faith and Science in an Unjust World*, still stand as monuments in the field of moral and spiritual responsibility in the interaction of scientific discovery, economic interest and political power.

I was involved in all of this. More of it will come up later, as the story of this adventure proceeds. But first, another involvement intervened. It was just as ecumenical, but it played out, not in world meetings, but in the life and witness of a church. After a summer in Geneva, we were sent as fraternal workers to Germany.

VI.   THE CHURCH IN GERMANY

1. Initiation: Mainz

It was a different, but related, world. Switzerland had escaped the devastations of conflict. It was orderly, and neat, an island of peace in a continent at war. One need only cross the border to see how exceptional this was. But at the same time Geneva, under the surface of civil order, was alive with networks that crossed battle lines, whether for intrigue, for rescue, for profit, for peace, or for faithful witness to Christ. The city was peaceful but not isolated, and, in the post-war years it was the hub of re-established relations. So it was natural that we, servants of one of these networks, the World Council of Churches of which the Presbyterian Church USA was a member, should be sent to serve a church recovering from the war.

We were assigned first to Mainz-Kastel, a suburb across the Rhine from the city of Mainz. The city was in ruins, 85 percent destroyed, they said. Rubble was everywhere. Only the cathedral, the University on the hill, and the palace on the Rhine were left standing, and the auditorium in the palace featured a large mural of the city in flames. But the people were friendly. Not only that, they welcomed us. One would expect that from fellow Christians, many of whom had been part of the Confessing Church in resistance to Hitler, but it was true generally. The Christian spirit radiated. One could bask in it, and we did. Our second child, Walter, was born there, in the loving care of a German hospital. We were personal friends with our hosts, Horst and Isolde Symanowski, who with their family had fled the Soviet army from east Prussia. We shared family prayers with them, and family experiences as well. We learned to love the German Gesangbuch, the hymnbook, cleansed of sentimental songs that had not helped them through Nazi times. We also lived with the Petzold family in whose crowded home we rented rooms, along with a group of friendly students who were also roomers. They were our friends too. From them all we learned German culture and German language, as they gently guided us and corrected our mistakes. Nor were we the only ecumenical workers in Mainz. On a hill amid the ruins (French occupation zone) was a barrack which housed CIMADE, a French Protestant movement that during the war had cared for refugees and hidden Jews from the Nazis. Now it was helping in the reconstruction of Germany. On our side of the river, also housed in a barrack, was the Gossner Mission, to which we were assigned.

Gossner was a unique Society. It started in the nineteenth century as a mission to Russia. Later it moved to India. After World War II, it opened a trailer church in the Soviet Zone of East Germany and soon after, a ministry to industrial workers in Mainz. The Mainz project was rooted in the alienation of labor from the Church over a century and a half of German history. Industrial workers were rarely seen in church. That was a place for the bourgeois establishment and for conservative politics. So when Pastor Horst Symanowski, director of Gossner Mainz-Kastel, applied for a job in a cement factory, it caused a sensation. It was also a way into ministry to workers and renewal of the church, which the Mission carried on for years. We lived with Horst, Isolde and their family for a year. We prayed with them, sang hymns with them, and worked with them. It was our introduction to German society and to the German church in process of repentance, witness and change.

There was a history behind all this. It stretched back centuries and in mid-twentieth century, still lived. We were in the middle of it, so it might be well to sketch the scene. It goes back to the Thirty Years War, 1618 to 1648, when Protestant and Catholic monarchs fought over the land. One third of all Germans died during those years and the country was devastated. Then came the Treaty of Westphalia in 1648 when, under the judgment of God, probably due to exhaustion of funds and energy, the princes made peace. The principle was that each ruler should determine the religion of his domain (*cuius regio, eius religio*), and support the church of his choice there. The result was Roman Catholic kingdoms (e.g. Bavaria) and, still in 1950, twenty-eight Protestant *Landeskirchen*, provincial churches dating from the seventeenth century. They were Lutheran, Reformed, or United, even though the kings, dukes and counts who ruled their territories had long since lost their power.

There were changes of course. First was the rise of Prussia in the nineteenth century. The Prussian king in 1817 did not care about

Lutheran-Reformed differences. He only wanted peace and control. So he decreed that there should be one church administration, but that congregations could be Lutheran or Reformed as they chose. When Prussia united Germany in 1870, the Roman Catholic Church was recognized and church taxes supported it also. So it was until the Nazi time. The church was disestablished in 1919 but the state still collected taxes (10 percent of income tax) and turned them over to the church (Lutheran, Reformed, United or Catholic) of which every German was a member unless she or he officially declared withdrawal.

Few did. Even Karl Marx was confirmed in a Lutheran congregation. His father had converted, primarily for social reason, so as to remove the (then mild) stigma of being Jewish. Most workers in industry were Marxists; they, like Karl, had little use for religion. But they still kept their church membership. Germany, in the early twentieth century, was full of "four wheel Christians," labor and bourgeois, who came to church once in a baby carriage for baptism, again in a coach to be married, and finally for funeral in a hearse. It was part of the culture.

Of course, the church also had its own vitality. In the nineteenth century, many foreign missionary societies besides Gossner were formed, and sent missionaries to Asia, Africa and the Pacific. The Innere Mission was formed, often staffed by Protestant Sister Orders parallel to the Catholics, to minister to the poor and disabled as well. Most of them were still operating when we arrived. Furthermore, Christians were active politically. A Catholic Center Party was formed, between the Socialists on the left and the Conservatives on the right. Some Evangelicals, as the churches of the Reformation were called, became Christian socialists, including, in his early years, the Swiss Karl Barth, who transformed the Evangelical Church theologically over his long career.

Then came Hitler. An Austrian, and therefore Catholic by birth, he made a concordat with the Vatican, which respected but restrained the Roman Catholic Church throughout his reign (though there were Catholics who were heroes and heroines of the resistance). Toward the Protestants, he took a more aggressive line. In 1933 he appointed an obscure pastor, Ludwig Müller, as national bishop. Through him, he cultivated his own form of anti-Semitic "German Christianity." Its principles were basically a reinterpretation of the Christian faith to conform with Nazi concepts of nation, race, and historical destiny. There should be one racially pure national church. Jesus could not have been a Jew, and Jews by race, even if they were Christian by faith, could not be ordained to the ministry. And, most offensive to the Christians I knew who had lived in that time, revelation was historically continuous. Hitler's power and the Nazi ideology were seen as the modern form of this revelation.

This created opposition in the church. Martin Niemöller led the way. His congregation in Dahlem, a part of greater Berlin, was a center of resistance to Müller and his "German Christians." Niemöller formed the "Pastors Emergency League" (it sounds more pungent in German: Pfarrer Notbund) of which the young Dietrich Bonhoeffer was also a member. Its first petition drew 3,000 signatures and its protests led to the Barmen Synod in 1934. The Barmen Synod did not aim to split the Evangelical Church but to call it to its true faith, against the errors of the Nazi appointed leadership. Its Declaration, affirmed by Lutheran, Reformed and United churches together, made one ringing confession: "Jesus Christ, as he is attested for us in Holy Scriptures, is the one word of God which we have to hear and which we have to trust and obey in life and in death." Therefore, they rejected the "false doctrine as though the church could and would have to acknowledge as a source of its proclamation, apart from and besides this one word of God, still other events and powers, figures and truths as God's revelation."

The rest of the Declaration flows from this. They rejected other false doctrines, "as though there were areas of our life in which we would not belong to Jesus Christ, but to other lords; as though the church were permitted to abandon the form of its message and order to its own pleasure or to changes in prevailing ideological and political convictions; as though the church, apart from its ministry, could give to itself or allow to be given to it special leaders vested with ruling powers, as though the state, over and beyond its special commission, should and could become the single and totalitarian order of human life, thus fulfilling the Church's vocation as well and as though the church, over and beyond its special commission, should and could appropriate the characteristics, the tasks, and the dignity of the state, thus itself becoming an organ of the state and as though the church in human arrogance could place the word and work of the Lord in the service of any arbitrarily chosen desires, purposes and plans."

All these rejections, grounded in biblical references, were placed in the context of a confession of the faith and witness of the church to Christ as lord and savior. It was the faith by which members of the German Confessing Church, lived and died throughout the Nazi regime.

The struggle was intense. The Synod of Barmen led to a church headquarters which claimed to be the German Evangelical Church, so recognized by the Ecumenical Movement and by congregations in Germany to which support was owed, both spiritually and financially. In some congregations, two pastors, one Confessing, the other "official," would announce competing hymns and invite the congregants to outsing each other. Dietrich Bonhoeffer was commissioned to run a seminary to train Confessing Church pastors (because the university theological faculties were closed to them). It lasted two years, then was closed by the Gestapo, though two books by Bonhoeffer, *The Cost of Discipleship* and *Life Together*, survived as world-wide monuments to this experience. Of the students and other Confessing Church pastors, some died in concentration camps or as conscripts on the Russian front. Others were imprisoned, Niemöller among them. They, and others who survived, were called to lead the Church after the war was over. They were our friends and mentors, in Mainz and in Berlin.

2. Berlin and the Church under Communism

We were destined, however, for Berlin, with its openness to the east. Thereby hangs another history, this time post-World War II. Germany was never intended to be divided. Roosevelt, Churchill and Stalin decided at their Yalta meeting in early 1945 to expel fifteen million Germans (including our friends, the Symanowskis) from the eastern part of their homeland, and to assign the territory beyond the Oder and the Neisse Rivers to Poland. They also decided on zones of occupation which the French, the British, the Americans and the Soviets would occupy, pending a final settlement. But the settlement didn't come. After three years of futile negotiations, the French, British and Americans merged their zones and formed the Federal Republic of Germany. The Soviet zone became, in their categories, the German Democratic Republic (GDR).

Berlin was a special case. Lying in the middle of the Soviet Zone it was divided at Yalta into British, French, American and Soviet sectors. The Soviet Union tried, short of war, to blockade Berlin and take it over in 1948, but the Western powers responded with a massive airlift that supplied the needs of the city until the Soviets backed down. The result, in the 1950s when we were there, was a wide open city. One could go anywhere in its bounds by public transportation. More important, people from the east could come into East Berlin, which the GDR had designated as its capital. They feigned business there and then came over to the west. So it was until the wall was built in 1961, and cut off communication between east and west.

There were difficulties. Two different governments held sway, with two different police forces. Two different currencies circulated, with different exchange rates in east and west. I was once detained by an East German policeman while carrying a package of Marxist literature to the west (it was cheaper in the east). He wanted to know where I got the East German marks to buy the books. Then he took me and my Indonesian companion to a building in East Berlin that had no identification, outside or on its doors within. There, my Indonesian friend was told he could go, but he said he would wait until I could join him. Then I was taken for an hour's interrogation by two men who also did not identify themselves. They quizzed me on my politics and I gave them theological answers. I told them I represented the church, not the government, that I was there for Christians in east and west, and that I would like to visit the churches in the east if permitted. They referred me to the East Christian Democratic Union, a satellite of the Socialist Unity (Communist) Party, then gave me my books back (well, some of them; they slipped in a book of soft pornography as ballast) and let me go. Such was my experience with the SSD, later known as the *Stasi*. I'm sure they have a file on me. I've never checked.

The church did not accept the political division of Germany as a church division. *Die evangelische Kirche in Deutschland* (The Evangelical Church in Germany) Lutheran, Reformed, United and Moravian Brethren was, as one church, a member of the World Council of Churches. It maintained its spiritual and organizational integrity and held its synods for all of Germany, alternatively in east and west. The hymnbooks were the same; the worship was similar, though more urgent in the Communist east; the groups in the church—youth, students, missions, men, women—shared, in different conditions, the same spirit. We moved from Gossner

Mission west to Gossner Mission east whose national director, Hans Lokies was also head of the Office for Church Teachers of the Church of Berlin-Brandenburg, which regularly sent teachers into East Germany to serve the churches there. I taught in the institute college that prepared them for this ministry—about China. We knew, as we moved from Mainz to Berlin, that we were part of one Christian community. Furthermore, we were welcomed in the east, not as foreigners, but as symbols of what they called *die Öie al*: the worldwide community of Christians gathered in the World Council of Churches which had sent us to them, and which supported them with their intercessory prayers and fellowship as they faced their life and witness in a Communist society.

But they gave us far more than we gave them. Let me introduce it with two examples. They come from the conferences the Ecumenical Institute, Bossey, held each year in Berlin for pastors and lay people in the Communist east.

(1) A group of middle-aged women were describing the material problems of daily life, food for the family for example, when the shops were only sporadically supplied, and one had to go from one to another, the care of children when both mother and father were compelled to work, family prayers and religious nurture when parents were grateful but exhausted. But they took all this as a challenge and a vocation. "Long live the grandmothers!" they said. And the rest of the week was spent exploring with us how, in faith, that challenge could be met.

(2) On another occasion, a group came with a special situation; they had discovered that their pastor was informing on members of the congregation to the police. That can be dangerous. There was a law against "incitement to boycott against democratic institutions." A careless critical remark, spoken in private but reported, could bring one before the court, and perhaps to prison. But the group treated it as a pastoral problem. What made the pastor an informer? Was it fear? If so, what caused the fear? Was it concern for his family? Was it a sin (most often sexual or monetary) that he wanted to conceal from the public? The members became the pastors; the pastor became the object of their care. They of course avoided saying anything to him that he would have to report, but basically they were concerned about him. They were creating a Christian community in spite of, and around him. All week we learned from them about this ministry, and tried to help them with it.

In the light of these examples (and they were typical of many we heard) we can understand University Pastor Johannes Hamel of Halle in the East, when he wrote in a West German journal: "Let me say it clearly to start with: it is a good, a precious thing to preach here in the East that Jesus Christ alone, Lord and Saviour, refreshes the weary and the suffering, that he has found the lost and strayed, that no one can tear them from his hand, or take from them the peace which their Almighty Father gives."[1]

Among such people we lived for two years.

There were problems of course. The principal one was *freedom from fear*.

There was reason enough for fear. Oppression was everywhere. Soviet occupying military secured the state, and Soviet advisers controlled its policy. The goal of the state was to convert the society into a model of the Soviet Union, in ideology, politics, and economic structure. To this end the secret police (the *Stasi*) established a network of informers, and claimed to know everything about you, even what you said and thought in private. There was, according to our tough-minded Christian friends schooled by resistance to the Nazis, about one chance in five that they did. But one never knew. There was always a chance that one could lose one's job, that one's children could be harassed or denied advancement in school, or that one could land in prison, as Hamel and his colleagues were, for three months in 1953.

That was the outer fear. There was also an inner fear. Many Christians, like the majority of East Germans, profoundly resented the Communists and the Soviet occupation. There was constant temptation to live in "inner emigration" toward an idealized West, and therefore to conform to, while cutting off, the society they were in. Hamel used the image of a fist balled in one's pocket. We were often asked, "How long must we wait, until you (the Americans) come and rescue us?" All this deepened fear. It left people prisoners of their own hatreds, unable to give a free witness.

How, then, does one overcome fear? Let me add a few examples to those above. A woman student, member of the Student Christian Movement (SCM) in her university, was called in by the authorities and told that unless she joined the "Free German Youth" (a Communist front), she could not be admitted to final exams. For

---

[1] Johannes Hamel, *A Christian in East Germany* (London: SCM Press, 1960), 30.

the sake of her family which depended on her, she joined, but continued, on the advice of her pastor, to be part of the SCM, and to pray. Finally, she could not stand the tension. She went to the authorities a few weeks before the exams and withdrew from the organization. The authorities were amazed, and tried to persuade her. Finally, she said to them, "Because I was afraid for myself I came to you. Because the gospel has taken that fear away from me, I am leaving now."

Another example: Johannes Hamel was himself imprisoned in early 1953. As he described it to me later, he was not physically abused, except for the conditions of his imprisonment (solitary confinement, poor food, and a single bulb burning 24 hours a day in his cell), but he was psychologically manipulated almost daily by interrogators who threatened and deceived him. At one point one of them asked him sarcastically, "Where is your Jesus now?" "Why," Hamel replied, "He's here. He's been here all along. I'm surprised you haven't noticed."

A West German pastor asked an East German colleague, "How free is your congregation?" The easterner replied, "We have as much freedom as we are willing to take." He had just held a youth rally in a local park. Christian instruction was given in his church, explicit in its repudiation of Marxist atheism. All such activities had their dangers. The three examples I have given turned out well. The student was admitted to the exams; she has exceptional character, they said. Hamel was freed and restored to his family. The pastor continued to function until the Berlin wall fell. But it could have been otherwise. Does one live in fear, or in faith?

A second problem was *truthfulness.*

There was reason enough to say whatever was required to get along, whether it was truthful or not. The government was seeking to impose an ideology on the whole society, the ideology of Marxism in a Stalinist form of Leninist interpretation, which led to uncritical support of Soviet foreign policy. The pressure was especially hard in the school. Children were not only taught ideologically; they were asked about their parents. "Dad, I lie every day in school," a boy said to his father, "If I didn't, you'd go to jail." But the pressure was on in the work place too, and in the public sphere. Every so often a referendum was held, "for peace," which denounced the Western warmongering powers, especially the

United States and claimed to speak on behalf of the "peace-loving" peoples of the world. Only a few resisted this hypocrisy by staying home, and they received visits that could be interpreted as persuasive or threatening depending on one's point of view. They might have consequences, or they might not. One never knew.

Christians were especially under suspicion, not only because they had a different faith, but because the church was the only social body not under the control of the Party. There, people responded to a different reality. There, a different standard of truthfulness prevailed. Martin Luther's emphasis on the word permeated the culture and made it difficult, despite—or perhaps because of—the Nazi experience, to prevaricate in order to get along.

This led in the churches to an intense study (continuous, for Confessing Churches, with resistance in the Nazi times) of the living word of God in Christ and the Bible. I was privileged to participate in many such studies. They took place not only among catechists who were allowed to gather children after school in church rooms for religious instruction (attendance at which was already a mark against the child and its family), but in congregations among its members as well. Each time it was an encounter with the reality of God among people who were trying to understand their history, their world, and themselves in God's presence. We talked about our relations with the Communists on several levels of truthfulness. There was the level of observed fact. Just pointing out that this work crew was behaving like an army with its shovels, or that women were not necessarily liberated by being forced to work in factories, could lead to trouble. There was the moral level. When could one deceive, or hide one's convictions in order to avoid conflict? When should one call hate or injustice by its name, in east or west, instead of excusing it by pointing to the evils of the other side? Then there was the question of faith. What is the relation of confessing Christ to Communist ideology? A few thought there was no conflict. Many regarded them as enemies. Most, however, wrestled with the problem: How can one bear witness to the truth of God's revelation in Christ in a society that dismisses religion and politically enforces its own humanist ideology?

That led to the problem of *justice*.

It is a Hebrew-Christian, not a Marxist concept, though Marxism arose and drew much of its strength from the injustice of early capitalist theories and practices. Marx and Lenin (and Stalin) spoke rather about the laws of history which led from a society where the vast mass of people were deprived of the fruits of their labor, and therefore of their humanity, until they rose in revolution, dispossessed their exploiters, and built together a classless society without private property leading toward communism. The Communist Party was considered the instrument of this revolution and the planner of the future, the enlightened mind of the masses, who knew the laws of history. This determined the law and the judiciary. "There is no crime apart from some harm to the people's progress toward socialism," said one official.

What does one do, when a neighbor is unjustly hauled into court for such a crime? The most general indictment was *"Boycotthetze gegen demokratische Insitutionen,"* incitement to boycott against democratic institutions, which meant the institutions of the "German Democratic Republic." Defense in the court is already a risk. Yet many Christians, church leaders among them, using older, Christian-influenced, standards of justice, did prevail in influencing judges, who were grateful for their support. One of the heroes of this legal struggle was Präses Lothar Kreyssig, a lawyer in the Provinz Sachsen (Magdeburg) Church who had brought a criminal suit against the Nazi government officials responsible for the killing of disabled children. The suit could not go forward and Kreyssig landed in a concentration camp, because it was disclosed that Hitler himself had given the order. Experience with the Nazis was good training for dealing with the Communists. Kreyssig among others, used it to the full.

Then there was the area of *social responsibility* in which all of this played out. Five–sixths of Communist East Germany was traditionally Protestant, overwhelmingly influenced by the teachings of Martin Luther. One of these, deeply ingrained in the people, was the belief that every occupation was a vocation, a calling, from God. This had its weaknesses as well as its strengths. It led often to a failure to see one's calling as a citizen beyond one's particular vocation. The Christian Germans we knew were shocked by Germany's failure to resist Hitler on this basis. There was much discussion when we were there, of the need to open the doctrine of vocation to broader responsibility in politics, economics and culture. But they were confronted with another demand on their sense of vocation, an atheist demand to serve the collectivized system whose model was the Soviet Union. The root of the conflict was the contrast between the practice of Christian vocation based on the teaching of Martin Luther and the government-engineered plan to realize the classless society by collectivized methods.

We heard almost daily of such conflicts. What does one do when one's farm is taken over by a Communist Party managed "cooperative" and one can no longer manage planting, cultivation and harvesting while at the same time being required to produce certain quotas of produce on schedule? One may recognize that the old system was unjust and needed land reform, but is this the alternative? Similarly, if one owns a business, small store or large factory, that is collectivized, and one can no longer responsibly plan purchases, sales, or production. To be sure, in the old system, profit played too large a role in these calculations, and workers were often exploited, but is total planning the answer? What does one do, if it is imposed?

What is responsible Christian witness in situations such as these? Certainly, to respond first of all to God's judgment and grace, to find one's hope not in tradition or ecclesiastical influence but in the victory of the risen Christ over the powers of the world. As one pastor put it, "When we talk with westerners, they tell us of the problems confronting them, and we tell them what is happening to us." Therefore, the church warned against finding salvation, or even justice, in either the solidarity of a centrally planned classless society or in the individualism of private enterprise, however attractive they may be as ideals. In other words, human problems cannot be solved either by the Communism of the East or the capitalism of the West, but by Christian hope and responsibility in both. This meant, for easterners, accepting from God, responsibility to "seek the welfare of the city" (Jer 29:7) that had been imposed on them, to work for "an improvable socialism" (to quote one church document), and to take responsibility wherever they could, even in collective enterprises. "Send me Christians," one Communist manager cried, "They're the only ones I can depend on." All this in the context of living freely and responsibly as witnesses to the risen Christ and the kingdom of God in a society where another ideology and another power claimed to reign.

3. Theological Transformation

We left Berlin in 1953 in the middle of all this, but the experience left me theologically and spiritually transformed. Never before had I prayed so fervently, or expected so much of God, as in those two years. My friends were living their faith, and challenging me to live mine. Shortly before I left, a group of Christian students asked me to talk with them about freedom. Because, they said, "You live in a free country. What does freedom mean for a Christian there?" I was almost speechless. That was the time when Joseph McCarthy was intimidating Congress and the government in the United States with charges of Communist influence, and powerful people were afraid to confront him. I told the group about that, and promised I would tell Americans about their freedom in Christ, confronted with far greater dangers than McCarthy. I hope they heard it. They may have, because forty years later I was sitting in a church in Leipzig, listening to the pastor tell a West German audience about his experience in 1989 just before the Berlin wall fell, with protesters massed inside his church confronting the East German Army outside. The same gospel was at work there.

It was also a theological transformation. I asked my East German colleagues what theologians they found most helpful, informing their ministry to their congregations and to the Communists. Their answer was universal: Martin Luther and Karl Barth. Luther I had read and studied, appreciatively and critically with Reinhold Niebuhr, more deeply and appreciatively with his brother Richard, but not nearly as deeply as my German colleagues, who consulted him weekly for his biblical and theological insight as they prepared their sermons.

Barth was another matter. He was contemporary, and principally known during my doctoral studies in the United States for the absolute discontinuity which he proclaimed, between human reason and divine revelation. His ethics in *Church Dogmatics* Vol. III:2 and III:4 had not been published yet. Richard Niebuhr told me that I need not bother with him in Christian Ethics, my doctoral concentration. But here he was, totally involved. He had been the author of the Barmen Declaration, adopted by the Church in 1934 as a confession of faith against Nazi Christianity. From his exile in Basel, he had inspired resistance to the Nazis as long as they lasted.

Now he was affirming, inspiring, and theologically informing the Church in a Communist land. I resolved, I had to read him.

A third theologian must be mentioned in this transformation, though his influence crept over me later and is still creeping: Dietrich Bonhoeffer. He had died, executed by the Nazis in the last days of the war, six years earlier. But I was invited in Berlin to join a radical group called the *Unterwegs Kreis*, many of whose members had been students of Bonhoeffer in Finkenwalde, his Confessing Church seminary fifteen years before. One of them was his intimate friend who married his niece and later became editor of the works he left, *Eberhard Bethge*. Bethge brought to *Unterwegs* the letters that Bonhoeffer had written him from prison from 1943 to 1945. I read them, and was enthralled. Bethge claimed that it was my encouragement that moved him to publish them. Well, perhaps I was one of the chorus. They appeared in 1953 as *Widerstand und Ergebung* (Resistance and Submission. *E.t. Letters and Papers from Prison*). I still have the copy I bought in Berlin then. It turned out to be the most influential German theological book of the post-war decades. Here was a Christian mind, faced with war and death, expressing himself unguardedly to a friend with all his learning and spirit, but without editors or scholars reading over his shoulder. The results were exciting. For example:

> (Advent 2, December 5, 1943) In recent months I have been reading the Old Testament much more than the New. It is only when one knows the unutterability of the name of God, that one can utter the name of Jesus Christ; it is only when one loves life and the earth so much that without them everything seems to be over that one may believe in the resurrection and a new world.

Or:

> (April 30, 1944) I should like to speak of God not at the boundaries but at the center, not in weakness but in strength, and therefore not in death or guilt, but in human life and goodness. As to boundaries, it seems better to be silent and leave the insoluble unsolved. Belief in the resurrection is not the 'solution' of the problem of death. God's 'beyond' is not the beyond of our cognitive faculties. ---- God is beyond in the midst of our life. The Church stands, not at the boundaries where human powers give out, but in the middle of the village.

Or, July 21, 1944, when the attempt on Hitler's life had failed and Bonhoeffer knew his fate was sealed:

I discovered later, and I'm still discovering up to this moment, that it is only by living completely in this world that one learns to have faith. One should abandon any attempt to make something of oneself, whether it be a saint, or a converted sinner, or a churchman (a so-called clerical type), a righteous man or an unrighteous one, a sick man or a healthy one. By this-worldliness I mean living unreservedly in life's duties, problems, successes and failures, experiences and perplexities. In so doing we throw ourselves completely into the arms of God, taking seriously not our own sufferings, but those of God in the world—watching with Christ in Gethsemane. That, I think, is faith; that is metanoia; and that is how one becomes a man and a Christian.

There are lots more, but these quotations will explain the excitement. It also leads me back to the family, to the trip home and to the interlude in England. The second year in Berlin, Ruth and I were expecting our third child. We were also, having been six and a half years overseas, overdue for furlough with the Presbyterian Church's Board of Foreign Missions, our employer. So we went home, but by way of England. During our time in Berlin we had continual contacts with Britain, not only with Oldham, but with the British Student Christian Movement as well. It was Oldham who introduced us to the Community of St. Julian's and to the memory of its founder, Florence Allshorn, whom he had known and admired. It was a community of former women missionaries who had been given a manor house in rural Sussex and turned it into a place of rest and recovery for missionaries and ecumenical workers such as we. Sisters took care of children separately in a house across a field where skylarks rose and sang. There was daily prayer of course—compline in the Anglican tradition—in which we joined. There was also breakfast in bed, and silence at other meals. But after lunch and dinner, we gathered in the parlor for fascinating conversation from around the world. There we met Canon Max Warren, leader of the British Church Missionary Society, by whose conversation and writings I was inspired, and read avidly from then on. Through Oldham I also met Ronald Gregor Smith, the Editor of the SCM Press who had passed my reflections on China to Oldham for comment. A wonderful friendship developed. Gregor Smith's wife was German; he was a friend of Karl Barth; and he discovered Dietrich Bonhoeffer about the time I did. We plotted the translation of the *Letters and Papers from Prison* together. He later, as a professor in the University of Glasgow, to the dismay of Barth, moved in the direction of existentialism. Barth sent him a post card which he showed me: "I hear that you are taking up existentialism. Don't! It's a blind alley."

From St. Julian's, I saw Ruth and the children off at Southampton on the Queen Mary. They went to New York, where our third child was born. I went back to Berlin for two months. We had hoped for a girl and had several names chosen. So it was a surprise on June 29th to get a telegram from Ruth: "Glenn Andrew West was born yesterday evening." It seems like yesterday, but Glenn is now 60 years old! It was a fascinating summer in Berlin. A group of us young ministers (all German, except me) studied hope, which was the theme of the coming Second Assembly of the World Council of Churches in Evanston Illinois, on which twenty-five world theologians were also working. We looked at it theologically and practically. What do people hope for, in East and West, and how is hope in the risen Christ related to it? Meanwhile, in June of 1953, East Berliners demonstrated *en masse* 1953 against the conditions of their life. There was hope in the air and it was exhilarating. It did not last. The Soviet troops in Berlin suppressed it. But it demonstrated the spirit of Berlin. Shortly after that I left for Geneva, carrying all that I had learned, and tried to communicate it to a Church and Society meeting that was preparing for Evanston, with indifferent success. Then home to New York.

VII.   COMMUNISM AND THE THEOLOGIANS: NICHOLAS BERDYAEV AND RUSSIA

I walked into the dean's office at Yale Divinity School after six and a half years' absence and declared my readiness to write a dissertation. "West," he said, "Choose a subject that is a thousand miles from your experience. That way, you will get it done." I did not take his advice. I was too full of the inspiration the experience of the last two years had given me. So I went to work on theologies that underlay the churches' encounter with the Marxist-Leninist form of Communism, in all their struggles and temptations. I first went to the original encounter, between Russian Communism and the Russian Orthodox Church and to Nicholas Berdyaev, the Orthodox philosopher who experienced it and wrote from exile about it. This led to my engagement with the Russian churches, which is the subject of this chapter. Then I turned to the Czech theologian Joseph Hromadka who accepted the Communist revolution and bore his Reformation centered witness in it. Then to Emil Brunner who spoke for many in the West for whom Communism was the enemy, and to Reinhold Niebuhr who, in his youth was a socialist and saw Communism distortion of it as a possible judgment on a sinful society. I included Paul Tillich whose "Religious Socialism" was an early attempt to include and transform Communism in a religious sense. It was crushed in Nazi power.

I studied Emil Brunner as an example of Communism as the enemy; Josef Hromadka who saw it as God's judgment on and promise for the Western world; Nicholas Berdyaev, the Russian Orthodox philosopher who interpreted it in reaction to, and corruption of the Russian soul; Paul Tillich who sought to understand its true depth as religious socialism; Reinhold Niebuhr who saw it as the violent judgment of God on capitalism but hoped for a repentant form of Christian socialism; and finally Karl Barth who guided the East German Church in its encounter with a Communist regime.

I was absorbed in this enterprise for nearly two years, with time out for visits to churches, conferences, Rotary Clubs and countless other meetings, wherever I could to deepen understanding of Christian witness to and in the Communist world. It was at great cost to my family (although we went on vacations together). I was in another world, not there where they were most of the time. My wife and my three sons have forgiven my absence since then, thank God. Without their support, and that of Ruth's parents who helped care for the children, I never could have done it.

Nicholas Berdyaev and Russian Orthodoxy

I started with Nicholas Berdyaev, who wrestled with Russian Communism before and after the Revolution of 1917. Although I had read Dostoyevsky, Turgenev and Chekhov, it was my introduction to the peculiarly Russian culture and the form of Bolshevism it produced. Berdyaev was a philosopher who was part of the Russian renaissance in the first two decades of the twentieth century. Then, as a refugee in Paris, he was a leading intellectual of the Russian Orthodox Church in exile. He was both an Orthodox Christian and a philosopher, on the frontier of encounter with the whole development of Russian thought, including the Leninist form of Marxism. More importantly, he was deeply Russian, but with enough experience in Western Europe to interpret his country to us. For example:

> In the west is conciseness; everything is bounded, formulated, arranged in categories, everything (both the structure of the land and the structure of the spirit) is favorable to the organization and development of civilization. It might be said that the Russian people fell a victim to the immensity of its territory. Form does not come to it easily; the gift of form is not great among the Russians. (*The Origin of Russian Communism*, Ann Arbor pb. 1960, p.9)

The result was, paradoxically, a totalism that resisted critical distinctions, such as that between church and state, interests in politics or religious pluralism even in Christianity. As he explained the extremism to which it led:

> The religious formation of the Russian spirit developed several stable attributes: dogmatism, asceticism, the ability to endure suffering and to make sacrifices for the sake of its faith whatever that may be, a reaching out to the transcendental, in relation now to eternity, to the other world now and in the future, to this world. The religious energy of the Russian spirit possesses the

faculty of switching over and directing itself to purposes which are not merely religious, for example to social objects. In virtue of their religious-dogmatic quality of spirit, Russians—whether orthodox, heretics or schismatics—are always apocalyptic or nihilist. Russians were true to type, both in the seventeenth century as Dissenters and Old-ritualists, and in the nineteenth century as revolutionaries, nihilists or Communists. The structure of the spirit remained the same. (*Ibid*, p.9)

Illustrations of this spirit abounded in my later experience. In a museum in Moscow celebrating the achievements of the Soviet Union, which I visited in 1962, there was a luxuriant sheaf of wheat enshrined on a platform in the middle of the room. It was intended not to show how farming worked but to glorify Soviet agriculture. The same was true of the other exhibits in the museum. Or there was the story a German prisoner of war told, of a truck carrying prisoners in a cold rain over a muddy road to a new location. The truck broke down, and the driver got under it to make repairs. As he emerged, covered with mud, he smiled and said, "*Nitchevo* (it doesn't matter). In forty years we'll have Communism" (a society where, according to Communist ideology, the state will wither away because there will be no need for it, and each will give according to his ability and receive according his need).

The same was true of the church. In Soviet times in Moscow, places of worship could not display any outward signs of their existence. They were shabby exteriors in shabby streets. But inside all was different. The splendor of an Orthodox church has to be experienced to be believed: the iconostasis in front of the nave with its icons of the saints set against an ornate background with candles lit by the faithful before them, the priestly robes, the deep resonant (a cappella) music, and over it all, the dome with Christ the Lord at its center. The liturgy spans history, from creation to the last judgment. It all says to the believer: Here is reality, whatever happens in the world outside. Priests and bishops said to us who came to them, "The world, including the Communists, is a part of this history. The reality celebrated in the Church includes them, though they may not realize it."

Then there is the cell of St. Sergius, the patron saint of Russia, in the Trinity monastery in Zagorsk. Around the cell is a series of pictures of the life of the saint beginning from when he went alone into the forest to withdraw from the world. The next picture shows the animals seeking his blessing. A third, a few monks coming to join him. The fourth, a monastery, the fifth, a city with the monastery at its center. The last picture shows the Grand Duke of Moscow with all his troops, coming to St. Sergius for a blessing before going to war against the Tatars.

All of this is rooted in Russian history. In the tenth century, the Grand Duke of Kiev, having established rule over the central part of Russia, reportedly invited representatives of the major religions to present their case to his court. In 988, he adopted Byzantine Orthodoxy. In the liturgy, "he felt he was in heaven," he was reported to have said. Thus Russia became Orthodox, but with a universal sense of its being and status. After the fall of the Byzantine Empire, Moscow claimed to be the "Third Rome."

So developed the Russian Idea, as Berdyaev understood it. For him the Russia which is of the spirit, Russia in the thought of the Creator, is not just a land, people and a culture among others, but the carrier of a saving mission for the world in its religious soul. This is not just nationalism or imperialism; it transcends all that. Berdyaev does not hesitate to speak prophetically to his countrymen on the basis of a lofty Christian vision of his land's vocation. He regards the Muscovite Czars—including Ivan the Great, Ivan the Terrible, and even Peter the Great—who reigned between 1547 and 1725, as perversions of the soul of Russia, combining state power with the conversion of souls. He sees the revolutionaries of the nineteenth century—the *narodniki* who idealized the people, the nihilists, and the Marxists—as rebels against Czardom but themselves victims of this combination of spirit with power. He identifies himself rather with the revolutionary spirit of Dostoyevsky who did not try to justify evil, but projected a vision of a profounder revolution of freedom and community. He confesses that he came to Christianity by accepting not the Christ of Scriptures, but the Christ who confronted the Grand Inquisitor in Dostoyevsky's novel: *The Brothers Karamazov* (published in *The Russian Messenger*, 1880). In short, he interpreted Russia as a culture that did not really distinguish between church and society. It saw them whole as suffused, even in revolt, by a divine reality and vocation.

Thus began many years of contact with Russian Christians, both before and after the collapse of Communism. This introduction helped me to understand and relate to at least the Orthodox part of it.

In 1962, my first visit to the Soviet Union was as part of a National Council of Churches USA delegation. The churches of the Soviet Bloc in Eastern Europe had joined the World Council of Churches in 1961, after years of negotiation. Delegations from member churches was the logical next step. But there was a third party to these negotiations: the government of the Soviet Union with which the churches in the Union had to deal. 1962 was the Khrushchev era. The churches having been freed from persecution as a result of their nationalist role in World War II, were now under new pressure. There was aggressive atheist teaching in the schools, churches were being closed and their publications limited and censored. Still, the interest of the Soviet government was clear and the church leaders used it. It was to cultivate friends among the Christians of the West and the Global South, and to use the churches of the Soviet Union, especially the Russian Orthodox Church, to do so. It had already infiltrated the Church with informers, and it demanded that the bishops and clergy of the churches report to it regularly. But the churches had another agenda: to use ecumenical contacts to increase the freedom of Soviet Christians to exercise their faith. We foreign visitors were willing servants of that agenda. The question for us was: How do we understand our Soviet Union hosts? Who was a believer, a nationalist, or a communist, and in what mixture? We assumed that everyone we talked with would have to report our conversation to the government, but what would they say? How would they understand us and we them?

Archbishop Nikodim, head of the Foreign Office of the Moscow Patriarchate (later Metropolitan of Leningrad), was the prime puzzle. He was a clever, jolly man, and the chief negotiator with the government for ecumenical relations. As such, he joined Josef Hromadka in the Christian Peace Conference (CPC) and pushed the Soviet foreign policy there, as well as in every World Council of Churches meeting he was part of. He used to give signals in such meetings to the Russian delegation, how to vote. I remember sitting with him on two occasions negotiating as chief spokesman for the Americans. It was hard-nosed diplomacy. On the other side, he slipped favorable documentation about a dissident priest in disfavor with the government, to a friend of mine who he knew would publish it. He opened doors for us and cultivated ecumenical contacts wherever he could. He respected our faith and our worship; but it was his love of the Orthodox liturgy that persuaded us that he was fundamentally a churchman. His negotiations with the government were on behalf of the church. Over time, recognizing the limits of his position, we came to trust him.

So it was with other churchmen and women we met. We participated in Orthodox and Baptist services and drank deeply of the faith of each. The Orthodox Church was rich from the sale of candles, with icons the only source of income. We heard stories of candles being burned in museums where holy objects were on display. To the question, how many believers are there in Russia, the standard answer was always given: wrong question. The Church embraces all the people, whether they recognize it or not. All are included in the drama of salvation which the liturgy enacts.

The next delegation of which I was a part, in 1974, featured the same characters, but it was quite different. Khrushchev was gone, overthrown in 1964. With him went the intense atheist educational movement and limitation of the churches that he promoted. The Soviet invasion of Czechoslovakia to crush the Prague spring had taken place in 1968 (see below) and with it the destruction of the Marxist-Christian dialogue. The leadership of the Soviet Union, whether from policy change or weakness, was more relaxed. We were invited to visit places (e.g. Talinn in Estonia and Riga in Latvia where there are Lutheran churches) that had been closed to us before.

More important, substantive dialogue, based on papers from both sides, took place between the churches in the Soviet Union (dominated by the Russian Orthodox Church) and the churches of the United States (arranged by the National Council of the Churches of Christ) which were discussed in open session. The theme was that of the World Council of Churches Fourth Assembly slogan: *Jesus Christ Frees and Unites*. The subject of my paper was "Implications for World Peace." I include it here.

VIII. "JESUS CHRIST FREES AND UNITES: IMPLICATIONS FOR WORLD PEACE"[1]

"And when Jesus drew near and saw the city he wept over it, saying, 'Would that even today you knew the things that make for peace!'"

Luke 19:42

There are two levels on which one can say that freedom and unity are the component parts of peace. It is a fact which the world understands in its own terms. It is also a statement of the life of the Church with Christ, and the promise of God for his world. It expresses the world's yearning; and it expresses the Church's mission. The relation between these two concerns us here. When the World Council of Churches took the theme: "Jesus Christ Frees and Unites," it committed the member churches to explore this relation so that out of it might come a proclamation in concrete terms of the way in which *Jesus Christ* is the source of peace among peoples and nations. But Scripture committed us to this exploration long ago. The city of Jerusalem over which Jesus wept did not know the things that make for peace, and it faced destruction because of it. Who is Jerusalem today? Is it not both the world and the church? The world of course has its own ideas of how the balance of freedom with unity brings about peace. Its varied understandings are based on various ideologies and interests; it is not hard to see how they lead to conflict with one another. But does not the church bear the greater sin if, knowing and confessing Christ as its head and its life, it still reflects the world's divisions and conflicts instead of showing Christ's peace in concrete terms to the world?

This, then, is our agenda. This paper will explore it in three parts: first, peace in freedom and unity as the world today understands it; second, peace, freedom and unity as we see them in Christ; and third, some suggestions as to the form of the Church's mission which arise from the interaction of these two.

---

[1] Paper presented at the discussions of representatives of the National Council of Churches (USA) and the churches in the Soviet Union during September 9–13, 1974.

I. The Peace of the City of This World

In the providence of God, all people seek peace. This is the first fact of created human nature from which we can start. Freedom is often an acquired taste; peace is a basic longing of every heart, and a condition of life itself. No one has put this so clearly than Augustine of Hippo in the 5th century CE:

> Whoever gives even moderate attention to human affairs and to our common nature, will recognize that if there is no man who does not wish to be joyful, neither is there anyone who does not wish to have peace. For even they who make war desire nothing but victory—desire, that is to say, to attain peace with glory. For what else is victory than the conquest of those who resist us? And when this is done there is peace....For every man seeks peace by waging war, but no man seeks war by making peace. For even they who intentionally interrupt the peace in which they are living have no hatred of peace, but only wish it changed into a peace that suits them better....And in the case of sedition, when men have separated themselves from the community, they yet do not effect what they wish, unless they maintain some kind of peace with their fellow conspirators. And therefore even robbers take care to maintain peace with their comrades, that they may with greater effect and greater safety invade the peace of other men....It is thus that pride in its perversity apes God. It abhors equality with other men under Him; but instead of His rule, it seeks to impose a rule of its own upon its equals. It abhors, that is to say, the just peace of God and loves its own unjust peace; but it cannot help loving peace of one kind or another. (*The City of God*, Bk. XIX, 12)

So it is also today. Those who turned nuclear fission into weapons of unprecedented destruction, sought peace. The first atomic bombs were dropped with the object of shortening a war. Those today who have developed nuclear weaponry and who have stockpiled nuclear weapons to the point where the USA and the USSR could each destroy the other many times over, on fifteen minutes notice, are seeking peace through security. Guerrilla fighters in Africa and Asia are making war on governments in their countries in the name of a new peace for their people which they seek. Even terrorists, who plant bombs, hijack airplanes, kidnap and murder children, and make suicidal attacks on peaceful communities, are proclaiming in their way that peace of their community is being denied.

Even the worst disturbers of the peace of the world, in Augustine's time and today, seek some vision of peace. It is fortunate that God has so made human nature, for it means that even those whose peace depends on dominating, exploiting, or even exterminating others, are forced to make compromises with others despite themselves, and out of these compromises some provisional peace emerges. Nuclear arms limitation talks and treaties are possible despite mutual fear and distrust; civil wars can end in truce, negotiation and coalition government; terrorists either destroy each other finally, or move toward a larger and more common strategy to achieve their ends. The very use of peace, however, distortedly perceived, as the goal of human striving, as the object of both freedom and unity among men, throws people into relation to one another, renders them mutually dependent, and limits the absoluteness of any nation's pride and power. Thus does God in his providence preserve this world as a somewhat human place.

Knowing this first fact, we can face a second: the peace of this world is a tenuous and unsteady peace. It is always a compromise of conflicting interests, hopes and visions. It is gained by a balance of power more because sinful men and nations find themselves more threatened by the destruction of war than because they love and trust those with whom they agree to make peace. It is always breaking down when one class or race or nation thinks it can improve its own peace by dominating another more completely. It is threatened continually by different visions of justice and the common good, each rooted in the special interests of one part of human society and projected as if it were universal. More often than not it is a false peace—the agreement of powerful nations to harmonize their interests at the cost of the weak and poor, or the control by one class or group of the power of army and police with which to repress the rest of the country. In this sinful world, human beings understand their own peace in ways that make it objectively necessary for them to deny the peace of others, to dominate and exploit them. Therefore, compromises are unstable. Agreements break down in new conflicts. The peace which is imposed by force is upset by its victims. The peace which is won by consensus is broken when one party feels strong enough to change its terms. There are standards of justice and law that limit this power and uphold the cause of the weak. But even these are ideological: they universalize the interests of one group over against another, while they offer a relative principle of moral judgment on the actions of that group.

Why, then, should the Christian church concern itself about the struggle of worldly powers for this kind of a relative, fragile, tentative peace? The answer lies simply in the demands of love—God's love for sinful man. The peace of God is not intended only for the church, nor does it reflect only eternity. The covenant of peace as it is given to the church in Jesus Christ, is intended also for the nations to be their hope and inspiration. The peace which the church proclaims in its gospel is always preserving, strengthening, criticizing, and transfiguring the various forms of peace which the powers of this world established among themselves. The statement of the Apostle Paul in his letter to the Ephesians—"Now in Christ Jesus you who once were far off have been brought near in the blood of Christ, for he is our peace, who has made us both one, and has broken down the dividing wall of hostility" (2:13-14)—applies not only to Jews and other nations of his time, but to conflicting classes and nations in the world today. In this hope it is our task as Christians to search the efforts at peace-making in the world today, for signs of Christ's transforming work of judgment and reconciliation.

When we do this, I suggest we find two movements of world events: First, peace is happening in our world, and there is reason to thank God for it. It is worldly peace; it is fragile; it is fraught with unresolved issues; but it is real. Let me simply list some of the events of the past few years which illustrate it:

- The United States and the Soviet Union have reached agreement on the limitation of anti-ballistic missile systems in a formal treaty and have made an interim agreement to limit offensive nuclear arms, of strategic capacity. They are in negotiation to limit further the armaments race between them.

- Egypt and Syria have reached agreement with Israel for an armistice which involves some withdrawal of Israeli troops from conquered land and provides for negotiation toward a more permanent peace in the Middle East.

- India, Pakistan and Bangladesh are at peace with each other, and the relations between them have never been more cooperative than they are today.

- Nigeria is healing wounds of civil war by real forgiveness and reconciliation which has brought the Igbo people once again into the full common life of the whole nation.

- Laos, after years of civil war, is now governed by a coalition government and most foreign forces have been withdrawn from her soil.

- The People's Republic of China has been seated as a member of the United Nations, and the generation-long cold war between it and the United States has been turned into a normal diplomatic relation strengthened by trade and good will on both sides.

- The German Democratic Republic is on the verge of normal diplomatic relations with many Western nations which have in the past refused to recognize it, and is now a member of the United Nations.

- Portugal has had a change of government and is now moving toward negotiation with the liberation movements in her colonies.

These events are not the peace of God. Each one of them has its ambiguity and its danger. There is an arms race in weapons *technology* between the USA and the Soviet Union. Arab terrorists still raid Israeli villages and the planes of Israel bomb Arab refugee camps in reprisal. Bangladesh especially, but the whole Indian subcontinent as well still faces large scale hunger and want. Millions are dying of starvation in sub-Saharan Africa, down into northern Nigeria. The civil war continues with little prospect of compromise or coalition in Cambodia and Vietnam. Tensions continue between China and the Soviet Union. The GDR has to struggle for its socialist identity against the infiltrating influence of the German Federal Republic to the West. There is as yet no peace between Portugal and the people of her colonies, and in Rhodesia and the Republic of South Africa, there are not even the beginnings of *metanoia* by the white minority regimes. It is easy to be cynical and to discern selfish motives behind every peaceful move. But the task of the church is not to be weighed down by human sin, but rather to discern the signs of

God's work, as he uses at times the wrath of men to praise him (Ps 76:10). There is, by God's providence, and despite the sinful fears and greed of human beings, a movement toward peace.

Second, the peace that this world claims to be establishing and securing is being met by a counterwave of profound suspicion and protest; and in this protest is the hand of God's judgment on those prophets and priests who: "have healed the wound of my people lightly saying 'Peace, Peace' when there is no peace" (Jer 8:11). The theme of the coming Assembly of the World Council of Churches is: "Jesus Christ Frees and Unites." The world finds it hard to unite and free at the same time. Where unity is enforced in the name of peace by earthly power, liberation becomes a movement which divides, but who is really responsible for the division? Where human beings demand unlimited freedom for their own capacities, whether as individuals, as business enterprises, as sovereign nations or as the "working people" of the world, the other people whom they exploit and abuse in their struggle for freedom unite against them, and finally the limits of God's creation itself bring their hopes to destruction. But who is responsible for this limitation of freedom? But let me be more specific.

There are in the world a large number of people who hold the reins of power in their countries and who regard a monopoly of that power, against the claims of people of other races, languages or cultures, as basic to their peace. There is order in such countries, but there is no peace for the excluded people who have no share in power, and the peace of the dominant group is tenuous and threatened. In some cases as in Northern Ireland, this peace breaks down into a nightmare of civil conflict. In others, as in South Africa, rigid police repression keeps order in the midst of fear. But the problem is much more widespread than these two extreme cases. Wherever large groups of people are excluded from a part in the government of their society, their peace is denied. The key to peace is empowerment of the excluded, and sharing of power by the dominant.

There is an increasing number of countries in this world where unity and order have been purchased at the cost of suppressing dissent both on matters of practical policy and on matters of ideology. Dissenters are not necessarily wiser or more responsible than those in power. There is a risk to public order in allowing dissent. The dissenter, however, is a witness to the fact that no person or group in power is wise enough to do without criticism and protest against their policies. A government that allows dissent is recognizing that God and not some human political agency is the ultimate judge of justice and peace. The government that suppresses dissenting speech, press and assembly is creating unity at the cost of freedom; and this is false peace. One can only be distressed therefore at the growing number of countries—Chile, the Philippines, and the Republic of Korea are the most recent additions—where this suppression is a fact. Dissent will not disappear because it is suppressed. Peace cannot be based on the coercion of the human spirit, because there is a God who liberates.

There are in this world, whole nations which are coerced into an order which serves the economic and political advantage of other nations. This coercion may be directly political, it may be by economic influence, or it may be a combination of the two, reinforced by cultural and ideological pressures. There is a case to be made for the limitation of national sovereignty in favor of international order. No nation—not even the USA or the USSR—has an absolute right to act independently in an inter-dependent world. But an order in which the welfare of some nations is subordinated to that of others is the oldest and deepest form of false peace in the history of human politics. It waits only for a moment of weakness to explode.

These are examples of peace sought in unity at the cost of freedom. Peace can also be sought in freedom at the cost of unity, and the results are just as disastrous. During the past generation, technologically developed nations, both socialist and capitalist, have raised their standards of living and expanded their economies at an unprecedented rate. Millions have experienced the liberating exhilaration of instant communication, of new machines to serve them, of new products to enjoy, and of endless amounts of cheap energy at their command. Problems of social injustice have been softened by an expanding economy that promised to include everyone. Development was to be the answer for the poorer nations of the world. Freedom collective or individual, was to be the key to peace.

It has worked this way. In fact the gap between rich and poor in the world has grown greater during this generation, and the rich have used their technology and organization to appropriate the resources of the poor. The rules of trade and finance favor those who already have wealth, and efforts to change them by international action have proved futile. Rich nations in the Global North cling to their technological style of life and their level of consumption. They identify their peace with the right to buy and use these goods and services. So the conflict between the rich and the poor grows more acute as resources reach their limit.

Resources are reaching their limits. This is perhaps the deepest crisis of all for the peace of our time. Mankind, especially those of us who do not belong to the masses of the poor, have broken the peace with God's creation in their greed for power and material gain. The imminent exhaustion of non-renewable natural resources for example, at present rates of consumption of mercury in thirteen years, tin in seventeen years, petroleum in thirty-one years and copper in thirty-six years—is only the surface of the problem. Substitutes may be found, but they require energy and all known sources of energy will add intolerably to the pollution of air, earth or water by smoke, gases, radioactivity or heat. Already, irreversible ecological changes have taken place in some lakes and rivers because of pollution and there is prospect that the same may happen to the oceans. Food supplies are facing a limit, and to expand them with increased fertilizer (needed to make new high yield forms of rice and wheat produce) requires again more energy. The world faces decreased natural resources, energy supplies, and food, with more pollution and destruction of the environment God has given us to tend. We have identified our peace with ever higher consumption of goods and expressions of power, and we are now caught in a warfare with created nature which mankind cannot win.

Real peace is being made in the city of this world. Reconciliation is taking place and justice is being realized in new covenants where unity is created by affirming the freedom of the members. These are worldly, provisional events but nevertheless they are signs of God's work. False peace is breaking down in this world wherever unity is attempted by force in violation of the freedom of others, and wherever freedom itself becomes the absolute value of sinful human beings. This too is God's work. Let us look at that work more directly.

II. The Peace of God

One can hardly do better than introduce this subject with quotation from The Consultation on Christian Concern for Peace in Baden, Austria in 1970, sponsored by the World Council of Churches and the Vatican through SODEPAX:

Peace for those who confess the Christian faith, cannot be defined simply as the absence of conflict, strife and war. The word shalom, as it is used in the Bible, expresses the wholeness of human life in a community of mutual sharing and affirmation. . . It includes prosperity, happiness, respect among friends, and all that belongs to personal fulfilment. For a community it means the flowering of its common life in all respects. It is the fulfilment of the promises of God. As such it is a dynamic concept which demands ever new realization in new personal and social situations. It includes not only the constant renewal and transfiguration of the individual man's outlook and inner being but also the constant re-examination and, if necessary, radical refashioning of the external social, economic and political structures of societies....

Peace is therefore inseparable from the achievement of justice in human life, provided that justice be understood in biblical sense, not as the administration of a set system of laws but as the activity of God, raising up the poor and outcast, vindicating the victims of oppression and saving men from their sins for new life with each other and with him. Justice means the establishment of the disadvantaged in the full rights and possibilities of their humanity.

One could hardly ask for a more concise or eloquent ecumenical statement of the meaning of peace for a Christian. It means for our purposes, I believe, the following:

First, the peace of God embraces the whole realm of human possibilities as God promises and intends them, here in this life and in eternity, in earth and in heaven, in the individual life and in society. It means liberation from all the dehumanizing forces which prevent this flowering of individual and community. Its quality is freedom.

It is wrong therefore to separate the spiritual peace of the church, and of the coming kingdom of God—peace with Christ and the peace of heaven—from the material peace which comes when we enjoy freedom, prosperity, and harmony in our time on this earth. When Jesus said to his disciples, "Peace I leave with you; my peace I give to you; not as the world gives, do I give to you," he was not offering a substitute for peace on earth, but a promise of it; "In the world you will have tribulation, but be of good cheer, I have overcome the world" (John 14:27; 16:33). In this sense it is quite legitimate to speak of a "struggle for peace." Because of the peace of God which is given to us in Christ, we are girded for the work of realizing his promise here in our world, against the powers of destruction, of idolatry, and of injustice. The Old Testament promises of shalom to the people of Israel is also the content of God's purpose for us today: prosperity—enough to live on and to live with, freedom from the control and exploitation of other people, and a deep communion of soul in which the fruits of love may grow between person to person and the finer arts of living may flourish. This we are to struggle for and cultivate, because God has given it to us. Archbishop Michael in his speech to the Fourth All-Christian Peace Assembly in Prague 1968 put it in eloquent words which I would like to quote:

> In its essence, the peace brought to earth by the Son of God, incarnated for our salvation, the peace sung by the angels and proclaimed by the word of God (Luke: 2-4), is not an abstract ideal, nor an object of pious but unfounded reverie. Peace is a gift that the Lord makes to man (Isa 26:12, John 14:27). Peace is the precious characteristic of the Kingdom of God (Rom 14:17). Peace is entirely real. This is proclaimed by the Holy Scripture of the Old Testament, and proclaimed by the Gospel and the prediction of the Apostles in their witness. The reality of peace as one of the divine gifts should be recognized and welcomed by Christians not in a static or weak contemplation, not as a passive reminder of the cases in which peace celebrated its victory or was won by enmity, but in active and contemplative movement oriented toward the aim, 'seek peace and pursue it.'

Second, the peace of God is expressed in the *relationship* of his covenant with us and our covenant with one another in him which limits and defines us as human beings. This is the unity which he intends and in which freedom has its meaning. Human beings are not self-creators; still less do they create God in their image. It is not promised that they shall expand their power and their possibilities to infinite dimensions. Nor are human beings mere expressions of a species, a class, or a nation, which claims its own absoluteness and immortality. Human beings are persons called into being by God as his creatures, given life, direction and promise at every moment by him. The limit on human freedom is at the very center of life, in our responsibility to the other person with whom we are to live and in the ultimate Other who is God. But this limit is grace, it is promise, and it is freedom if we 'lead a life worthy of the calling to which you have been called, with all lowliness and meekness, with patience, forbearing one another in love, eager to maintain the unity of the Spirit in the bond of peace.'" (Eph 4:1-3)

The paradox of this covenant relation is fundamental. This is why there can be no peace in the long run based on private liberties, rights and property alone, necessary as the protection of these may be against the power of government or of the majority. No one is free from the responsibilities which his relation to others and to God requires. It is also why governments, or indeed other social units including families, which try to maintain peace by enforcing unity by coercion are sowing the seeds of chaos. No order is secure unless it can be based on a true covenant, in which people, especially people in power, listen to, and are limited by, their response to others who share in the society. Unity and freedom are both re-defined by the personal relation which God's covenant establishes among human beings. Peace can only emerge from the dialogue and the mutual limitation which this covenant means. This is true not only for the church but for the world in its politics as well.

Third, the peace of God is a gift of the crucified and risen Jesus Christ to the world. It is not something which we human beings create or earn by the virtue of our lives or our politics. The peace of the world always breaks down in new conflicts. It always expresses the selfish interests of a dominant group, and therefore it always brings forth opposition. Even the people of Israel, even representatives of the Christian Church, have confused these two levels of peace. Both Pilate and the Sanhedrin crucified Jesus in order to keep peace in Palestine. Christ makes peace among men by opening up a new possibility for people caught in their sinful distortion even of the covenant promise of God himself—the possibility of the forgiveness of their sins, of repentance and a new relation with God and the neighbor. In the world people make peace by compromising with an enemy; it is Christ alone who overcomes enmity. It is he who disarms the power with which we destroy the very peace we try to enforce. It is he who frees us from that most tyrannous of all oppressors, our individual and collective selves.

This is the real gift which the church has to make to the peace of the world: the proclamation of forgiveness, freedom from our sinful selves and from all the powers rooted in human greed and pride which have enslaved us, and a new covenant in his body and blood. This new relation is possible not just for the church but for the world. It can be good politics to renounce power and dominance, to admit wrongs done by one's country, to trust others in a relationship which one does not control because, in fact, Jesus Christ has overcome the world. "If holy penitence is the best means of recovering peace of the soul," said Archbishop Michael in the speech mentioned above, "many and various means can become necessary for finding the lost peace among men."

Fourth, the peace of God is constantly upsetting our human peace. The struggle for justice is the name of this upsetting: the claims of others who have been excluded from our covenant and who do not share in our peace. But the justice at work here is not just some legal structure of rights: its goal is not just equality. It is the justice of God who reaches out for who are poor, who are disadvantaged, who are weighed down by their poverty, their sickness, their spiritual depression, or by their sin, and justifies them. It is a never-ending transformation of human beings, human relations, and of society. Let me again quote the Baden report:

> The establishment of peace through justice is never a finished task short of the coming of the new heaven and the new earth in the kingdom of God. The death and resurrection of Jesus Christ, our faithful and joyful new life with the risen Lord every day, and the promise of the coming kingdom indeed makes it both possible and imperative to work for peace realistically and with hope amid the conflicts of our time. The peace of the city of God bears upon and inspires the peace of this world, but the peace of this world is never identical with it. There is no ideal society. There is never a time or place when the problems of human conflict are essentially solved, when order is basically just and needs only to be improved. In every social and political system, it will be the task of peacemakers to make the cause of those who are denied justice their own and to help them to their rights, as well as to cooperate with all those forces of whatever faith or ideology which are seeking to build a just society. This is true for Christians and others when they are in positions of authority and responsibility as well as when they are not. Those with power and authority need constantly to be aware of their own bias and limitations, and to reappraise the responsible exercise of their calling and office.

In short, the peace and justice of God judge and transform our human political ideas of peace and justice continually. The way to peace in this world which is always open to the peace of God is the way of repentance and transformation, the way of seeking out and including in our covenant those poor and disadvantaged whom God has found before us and whom he is raising up.

Fifth, in the course of realizing his peace, the action of God may *create* conflict in human society. "I have come," said Jesus "not to bring peace but a sword." So it has proved to be where the gospel has been at work. Unchallenged evils are brought to light and pressure to change them builds up. The prophets of Israel were in a sense disturbers of the peace who organized parties around their condemnatory sense of how the word of God was at work in the society. In the midst of this conflict the church will be an advocate for the poor and those who have been denied their peace. It will take sides, as the World Council of Churches has in giving medical and educational assistance to African liberation movements, or as the Roman Catholic Church in Chile and in the Philippines has in bringing judgment on the unjust imprisonment of dissenters and the abuse of public trust by the governments there.

Here, an important question arises: how does the witness of the church differ from the political action of a dissident worldly opposition? The answer, I believe, lies in the character of the church's advocacy: it creates conflict in the name of the peace of God. That means that this advocacy is never simply solidarity with this or that revolutionary army, never simply hatred for those in power. It is the judging and saving message of Christ *for* the victim of injustice and for his oppressor as well. The conflict created is between God and the oppressor, and the faith is that his power will overcome not only the power of the oppressor but the vindictiveness of the victim as well, thus creating a new covenant of peace.

Finally, the peace of God is completed in Christ's reconciliation of all people, "not counting their trespasses against them" (2 Cor 5:19). The presupposition of reconciliation is justification—the transformation of the sinner by grace, and the vindication of the victim of injustice. The fulfillment of justice however, is in reconciliation. No human cause is absolutely just. No political movement, no oppressed people, no exploited class, struggling for justice, deserves to triumph absolutely, and to destroy completely all the power against it. God does not bring peace by any victory but his own. In this world the goal of every struggle for justice is a new relationship, a new covenant, a new mutual affirmation by those who once were enemies, in which *both* sides are transformed and find a new responsibility for each other. Thus does Christ win his victory over the principalities and powers of this world which seek to absolutize themselves, and thus does he bring his peace to bear on the world.

III. Consequences for World Peace

How, then, can this peace of God be made concrete in this world? Here each of us must take the risk of being very specific, even though it involves the risk of being mistaken. Let me, then, in the risk that God's forgiveness and the fellowship of the church makes possible, venture some thoughts on four specific issues.

1. Relationships between the United States and the Soviet Union are, praise God, improving. This improvement is fragile, as the peace of this world always is, based in common interests and threatened by fears and ambitions on both sides. A total ban on underground nuclear testing has not been achieved. Weapons technology, notably the development of Multiple Independently Targeted Re-entry Vehicles (MIRVs), is threatening to wipe out the single most important deterrent to nuclear war in a sinful world—the "second strike" capacity of a nation attacked by nuclear weapons, capable of destroying also the attacker. Military expenses are preventing peaceful development of the economy, and a new escalation is in sight despite the few agreements that have been reached. If present trends continue, including the spreading of nuclear weapons technology to other countries, the world will be a far more dangerous place a few years hence than it is today, just *because* every nation, and first of all the USA and the USSR, is driven by fear to seek security through ever stronger weapons.

   What can Christians do? I suggest the following:

   (a) We can speak out, in the name of peace and of security itself, for a military balance of power based on mutually agreed reductions of nuclear and conventional armament. No nation has a right to be so strong that it can destroy another. The argument that it will not use such strength will never convince anyone else. This means in a nuclear age that no nation can be secure against any possible threat. One of the greatest dangers to world peace is the type of military (and civilian) mind that determines the defense policy of a nation—not on the basis of a possible enemy's real intentions but on the basis of what that enemy could do if it were populated by devils instead of human beings. A certain understanding of each other, a certain minimum of trust for one another is absolutely essential for national security itself, and it is the key to disarmament.

(b) We can build relationships and mutual understanding which will give each of us a positive stake in the life of the other. This involves a risk of course. As we get to know each other better we cannot be indifferent to the internal conditions in each other's countries. It is natural and right for members of the Communist Party of the Soviet Union to be concerned about the freedom and civil rights of Communists in the United States. It is natural and right for American Christians to be concerned with the freedom of Christians in the Soviet Union to practice and to propagate their faith. Internal conditions in our countries are a factor in world peace. But this is a risk we must take if we are to build peace. Only by a crucial and sympathetic understanding of one another, only by listening to one another, can the relationships be built which will undergird the present delicate detente that is based on the compromise of interests and the fear of nuclear destruction.

2. We have an opportunity in the Middle East today to move toward peace between Israel and the Arabs. The way is still beset by dangers, but one important breakthrough has been made: enemies who until recently had been absolutizing their own righteousness in utter hatred of or contempt for each other, have reached an uneasy truce and have agreed to negotiate. How can Christians help those negotiations to succeed? I suggest the following:

(a) We can translate into political terms the biblical insight that the hope of the future which God is preparing for us is far more important than nursing resentment for past wrongs. No one can unravel all the injustices that have been committed in the Middle East by all parties during the past generation. Without some political equivalent of forgiveness, no future is possible. But in Christ God has forgiven our sins. Because he is Lord also of Jews and Muslims, there is hope. It is not for us of course to commend our religion to them. Christianity itself has too much to repent of in that part of the world, to proclaim itself as savior. But there is forgiveness, this we know in Christ. Therefore, compromise and new community is possible.

(b) We can be friends of both Jews and Muslims and become ourselves a link in the future reconciled community. Some Christians are Arabs. Some are Jews and all of us are heirs to the promise of Israel. At the risk of inner struggle with this almost intolerable tension, we may be called to live out first of all among both peoples, the reconciliation of Christ.

3. World social justice is a more urgent imperative than ever before, yet in our countries less attention is being paid to it. The gap between rich and poor nations measured in economic terms, is steadily growing. But the question is not just economic. It is a problem of the powerless of the poor and weak peoples to resist the economic, and sometimes the military, pressures of the rich and strong. The poor lack freedom to develop in their own way. Their leaders are bought off or manipulated by political pressure. Their raw materials or the products of their industry are channeled to richer nations at discriminatory prices. Their culture is invaded and distorted by the values of an alien country. In this situation, I suggest three emphases which the Christian church might make.

(a) We can help to make our fellow countrymen in the technologically developed, relatively prosperous world *aware* of the problems of the poor, and of the way our prosperity depends on them. We can humanize the relationship. It used to be that the poor were always near us. We could see them and they were on our conscience. Now it is the task of the church to create a spiritual nearness that will not leave our consciences alone, and to spell it out in terms of economic relations.

(b) We can welcome the power of the poor when it expresses itself, even when our prosperity is hurt thereby. It is said that other raw material producing countries are now organizing along the lines laid out by the oil producing countries recently, in order to bargain more effectively with the countries that need these materials. This is God's judgment helping to create a rough justice among us. Other countries have long played off the competitive interests of the world's great powers, moving closer to one sphere of influence now, and another later in order to gain more freedom of action over against them all. Again the rough justice of God is at work. Only when the poor are powerful enough to force our respective nations to consider their interests, will greater and finer justice be done.

(c) We can strengthen those forces of interdependence in the world which are truly international and do not depend on one great power or another. We can support the United Nations and try to give it power to work in its international aid and technical assistance programs and its peace-keeping operations especially. We can champion the cause of the seventy-seven less developed nations in the United Nations Conference on Trade and Development, leading to international trade policies that will protect poorer nations against the economic power of the rich. Independence is not the final answer for any people. But the channels of interdependence must be those in which all people really participate with power to affect decisions. On *these*, international community *is* built.

4. We are losing the struggle with ourselves to live within the limits of God's created world. The destructiveness of nuclear power is only the most immediately dangerous example of this. The limits of natural resources, energy production, and pollution all remind us that destruction awaits us because of our success in dominating nature and making it serve our ends. What can Christians contribute to peace with nature?

(a) We can take the lead in suggesting a quality and style of human life where progress and hope does not depend on an ever-expanding consumption of material goods. This does not mean transferring human hope to heaven. It means recovering the original intention of God for mankind that he should find his hope and his new horizons in exploring fellowship with God and his neighbors and should use his physical environment to express that harmony and promise. It means discovering how to bring forth the fruits of creation without destroying it. It means using technological and scientific powers as stewards and not as masters.

(b) We can seek to humanize technology itself, so that it serves ends that human beings in their freedom choose and not ends dictated by the system itself. There is no reason why every new scientific discovery—for example in the genetic determination of future generations, or the use of drugs to control human personality—should be used just because it is made. There is no reason why man has to fly faster than sound, just because it is possible. Science and technology are not absolute goods in themselves. Unless we decide in the light of a more humane and loving goal how best to use them and when to renounce them, the destruction they will bring on us will be the judgment of God.

(c) We can seek to make economic decisions serve, in the long run, general human welfare and not in the short run, interests of the few or the many. Whether our economies result from government planning or the operations of the market, we must bring them under a control that considers the full cost of production—in damage to the environment and use of irreplaceable resources and production of wastes for example—in the decision where to put priorities. We must consider future generations as well as our own, even though they cannot yet make their influence felt. We must give priority to the basic needs of the poor over the demands of the rich or of powerful governments for more complicated and expensive machines. Economic decisions are human decisions. They too express our obedience to the promise of God for human life, or our vain pursuit of our own greed and power out of which warfare grows. It should be the task of the church to help discern which is which.

IX. INTERACTION WITH THE RUSSIAN ORTHODOX CHURCH

Thus my contribution to the Moscow meeting. This led to a fruitful exchange, for which our friends from the churches in the Soviet Union expressed their gratitude in private conversations. I think they fed on our theological and ethical reflections which were not available in their restricted ideological environment.

But we went a step further. We decided beforehand that we would ask for a dialogue with Marxist philosophers. The officials of the Russian Orthodox Church were taken aback. They would ask, but they weren't sure it was possible. But then Metropolitan Nikodim took over. He saw it as an opportunity. It was arranged. We put a group of learned Marxists through their paces from an angle they had never heard before, and Nikodim sat grinning the whole time. He wasn't the only one enjoying it. At the farewell dinner for our delegation, several of the philosophers turned up and sought us out to continue the conversation. One of them later sent me a book which was a critique of my book, *Communism and the Theologians: Study of an Encounter.*[1] I still have it, but it is in Russian so I can't read it. Maybe I will meet Yuri Levadha in heaven where we will understand each other in God's language.

We went home but it was not over. The church leaders in the Soviet Union wanted to continue the conversation—in the United States. Already in Moscow a group of two Americans (Bruce Rigdon and myself) and two Russians (as I remember Rev. Vitaly Borovoy of the Russian Orthodox Church and Rev. Alexander Bichkov of the All-Union Baptists and Evangelicals) drew up a plan, including four papers and Bible study in small groups where we could talk informally. I wrote a letter to the President of Princeton Theological Seminary, James McCord, asking whether the delegation might be invited as guests of the Seminary in Princeton. The answer was immediate: Welcome! He consulted with Claire Randall, general

---

[1] Charles C. West, *Communism and the Theologians: Study of an Encounter* (Philadelphia: Westminster Press, 1958).

secretary of the National Council of Churches, who was arranging the trip and made arrangements to accommodate some twenty Orthodox prelates, plus Baptists, Armenians, Lutherans and others, with interpreters and American invited guests. The meeting was held at Princeton Seminary in March 1975. It was a successful meeting in several ways. There was a reception for the Seminary faculty, a public meeting for students and visitors, Bible study in small groups introduced by an American and a Russian leader, and even a protest demonstration organized by Carl McIntire. But first, in my memory, was the person and performance of the Rev. Vitaly Borovoy, Protopresbyter (the highest rank available to a married priest in the Orthodox Church) of the Russian Orthodox cathedral in Moscow. He was the leading theologian, the best communicator and the most creative thinker that we met. I had met him in Moscow twice and seen him perform at the World Conference on Church and Society in Geneva in 1966. The issue was Marxist-Christian dialogue which at that time was at its height in Europe. The overwhelming majority from all continents was in favor of the World Council of Churches promoting it, but the Russians were against it. A heated discussion took place, and finally Fr. Vitaly spoke up: "I will tell you why my brethren are so opposed to dialogue," he said, and then explained tactfully that they had not been able to study Marxist-Leninist doctrine and therefore could not intelligently discuss its relation to Christian faith. We all knew the conditions in the Soviet Union. We knew what he was saying. The confrontation passed without incident. His last assignment was as representative of the Russian Orthodox Church on the staff of the World Council of Churches.

This spirit was reflected also in Princeton. We wanted the students to have a chance to interact with the Soviet church visitors. This was difficult because many of them did not speak English (though we recruited as many interpreters as we could). But Fr. Vitaly had learnt enough English by then. He spent hours talking to students in the dorms about the experience of being a pastor in a Communist country; about officials who would argue with him and then come to church, hiding behind a pillar so no one would recognize them; about weddings and baptisms below the soviet radar; about informal education of youth in a country where church education was prohibited; and pastoral care in an atheist-dominated land. He inspired them and educated them.

The students responded, not only to Father Vitaly but to the whole visit. They entertained the members of the delegation in lounges after the evening sessions. And they engaged the students who came from Carl McIntire's seminary in Pennsylvania with placards to protest. They arranged with those students a discussion led by one of their faculty members and me. I was looking forward to it, but it never happened. Their seminary forbade it.

This was the first, and in some ways the most important, fruit of the visit. The second was substantive discussion of the theme: *Jesus Christ Frees and Unites*. There were two papers from the Russian Orthodox side. Bruce Rigdon dealt, for the Americans, with the Freedom theme. I dealt with Unity. It was the only faith and order theme this ethicist dealt with in his life but it was relevant to the life of faith. Since it has never been published and since it summarizes my appreciation of and questions to the Orthodox Church in Russia at that time, I include the first, unpublished, part of it here.

Jesus Christ Unites

Brothers and sisters in Christ. Nothing becomes more evident when this affirmation is made than that we are at a loss to explain how it is so. We are gathered as Christians from the republics of the Soviet Union and the states of the USA because we believe that Christ has brought us together and requires of us that we explore more deeply the community we have in him. Yet we know that in every expression of our faith—in worship, in theology, in mission and in service—our differences cleave into the center of that community. This is so not only because we are of different communions which cannot fully accept each other's ways of being the church, but also because we are Christians out of the experiences and loyalties into which our churchly existence has been woven in ways we seldom fully realize. Jesus Christ unites us. This is the confession of the World Council of Churches as it looks toward its Fifth Assembly in Nairobi. It is also our confession, and the reason why we are visiting one another. In confessing him we are divided; to obscure that fact results either in fine phrases that mean nothing, or in imposing on the ecumenical movement someone's—too often Protestant—understanding of our unity.

To explore this paradox, and to suggest some of the ways in which we might move beyond it, is the purpose of this paper.

It must be a modest purpose. Protopresbyter Vitaly Borovoy was right in pointing out, in his closing remarks to our meeting in Moscow, that more can be achieved in bilateral inter-confessional discussions toward theological consensus than in a mixed group such as this, of Christians from two countries. Much fruitful theology has been done in such meetings already, and one fruit of this discussion may be to promote the present enterprise. The World Council of Churches Department of Faith and Order has done much on the problems of baptism, the Eucharist, and the ministry, about which we should learn, but which we cannot duplicate here. Nevertheless, we have together a unique task. We are not delegates to a convention; we are church people visiting one another at home. We are exploring each other's lives in all their confusion and varieties, in all their mixture of what it means to be Orthodox, Baptist, Lutheran, Reformed, Russian, American, Latvian, Armenian, Black, white or some other color, in all the combinations of these and other determinants of the way we express ourselves as Christians. Here, in this mixture, we seek to discover what it might mean that Jesus Christ unites. We cannot do this just within one country. You, our Soviet friends, help us as Protestant and Orthodox in the USA talk to and share with one another by bringing the perspective of another society with different relations into our midst. You help us to become aware of the Americanism of our Christianity in all its forms and to gain the perspective of the faith we share, upon it.

Writing in *The Ecumenical Review* in the autumn of 1969, his Eminence Metropolitan Nikodim gave two reasons for the participation of the Russian Orthodox Church in the World Council of Churches: "Firstly, love of the brethren who feel how baneful are the divisions between Christians, and who declare their desire to eliminate the obstacles to fulfilling the will of our Lord Jesus Christ 'that they may all be one' (John 17:21). Secondly, awareness of the importance of coordinating the efforts of all Christians, in their witness and service to people in the complex conditions of the secularized world of today, subject to rapid changes, divided, but aspiring to unity." [2] More recently his Holiness Patriarch Pimen has reaffirmed these points:

---

[2] Metropolitan Nikodim, "The Russian Orthodox Church and the Ecumenical Movement," *The Ecumenical Review*, 21 no.2 (April, 1969), 117-118.

The Russian Church wanted the WCC to be an objective and effective forum for meetings and dialogue for all Churches and all Christians in their efforts at promoting, achieving, or rather restoring, the unity of all Christians in the One, Holy, Catholic and Apostolic Church; this process was to be simultaneously accompanied by vigorous cooperation on their part in serving the cause of peace throughout the world, social justice and brotherhood among all nations and people. These two fundamental aims—restoration of Christian unity and service to humanity—were and still are the basic goals behind our Church's participation in the ecumenical movement.[3]

I would like to base my remarks on an expansion of these two reasons, which I take to be, not just expressions of Christian activity, but essential to the very being of the Church.

First, Christ unites his church, and the ecumenical movement, whether in the World Council of Churches or in such relations as that which we express here between the churches of the Soviet Union and the churches associated in the National Council of the Churches of Christ in the USA, can be an instrument of that work of unity. Unity in Christ, in his one church, around his table in the Eucharistic communion he provides, is the reality both of our origin and our goal. On this we agree, and therefore we cannot fail to speak of it and to seek its realization whenever we meet together as Christians.

On the other hand, we do not have this unity. Not only this, we cannot reach an agreement on the character of the ecclesial reality which the ecumenical movement represents or the form of the unity we seek. The Toronto statement of 1950 remains the basis of a realistic assessment of where we are: "Membership in the World Council of Churches does not imply acceptance of a specific doctrine concerning the nature of church unity." A number of attempts have been made to say more than this, notably in the Toronto document itself, in the New Delhi Assembly, at Montreal in 1962 and at Louvain in 1971. But, as Metropolitan Nikodim makes clear, speaking for the Russian Orthodox Church, they have all been too Protestant. They have presumed too much. We recognize each other as Christians. We know that there is a special reality to our fellowship and our collaboration which is not shared by all human beings. We can express this reality in praying for and with one

---

[3] *Journal of the Moscow Patriarchate 1974*, no.8, 18.

another, in searching the Scriptures together as we are doing here, in learning theology from each other and in common service to our Lord.

In short, we recognize each other's confession of Jesus Christ as sincere, and Christ's relation to each other as that of lord and believer.

We yearn actively for the unity which he offers and provides. Yet every effort to express that unity, even in tentative form as a basis for further work, breaks down. As Fr. Meyendorff pointed out in his address to the Louvain meeting, even if we reach agreement on a verbal formula, we can be sure that it will be differently understood in our different churches.

Is there a way forward beyond this impasse? Why are we able to recognize each other as Christians but not as churches? What follows is not the work of an expert in the field but simply of a Christian in the Reformed tradition trying to understand division and to find the paths of Christ-directed community. Let me suggest that our problem is created by the fact that our various Christian experiences—sometimes in contrast to the professions of our learned theologians—locate the center of the church in different places. However broadly, then, we make room in our understanding for the emphases of other experiences, we draw back from each other when we express most deeply and personally our apprehension of Christ's presence. Whatever doctrinal agreements are reached in ecumenical conferences tend to fall apart when we take them back to our churches because the central experience of these churches with Christ does not change to express the broader reference. The reality of the church to each of us is too compelling to allow for an easy pluralism. This is why such visits and exchanges as the present one are so terribly important. Only by sharing one another's life of worship and witness at home in each other's churches can we move toward those changes in experience which will open new possibilities for the unity we seek.

Nevertheless, we are theologians. God has given us minds with which to respond to him, to question ourselves and each other, and to find among ourselves the fellowship he gives. Let me suggest that one profound sign of the working of the Holy Spirit among us is that none of us—and here I dare to include our Orthodox brothers and sisters—has defined the church from our own center to our own complete satisfaction. Our differences are fluid; they are questions to each other. And this mutual questioning is part of our self-discovery. Let me illustrate with three examples.

1. No ecclesiology is more disturbing, not only to our Orthodox friends but to Anglicans and Catholics as well, than that which understands the church primarily as an event, as something that happens in personal or social experience rather than something that is. Yet no ecclesiology has contributed more in the past century to the missionary outreach, to the drive toward ecumenical unity and, paradoxically, to the division of the church, than this. The heart of this experience of the faith is that the existence of the church is in order to fulfill its mission. It occurs in actual. This may have what is loosely known in this country as a conservative evangelical expression: Christ converts the individual soul and the saved gather in a congregation to await the coming judgment while seeking to bring others in. It may take a radical political form: the church must die as an institutional form in the old and unjust order of society in order to be reborn as a participant in Christ's revolution, transforming the world. It may express itself simply as impatient ecumenism, eager to see in the experience of togetherness in a World Council of Churches assembly or in such a meeting as this, the prophetic vision of the heavenly unity to come and the only church that really matters. In all of these expressions it is the event that counts, not the institution. Church happens where Christ is at work, in the saving of a soul, in a movement for revolutionary liberation in society, or in an ecumenical encounter where his transcendence is taken seriously.

   To describe the type is to underline its shortcomings. From the beginning of the ecumenical movement, more catholic and Orthodox churches have rightly pointed it out. In their rush to appropriate the event of the church, these evangelicals, individual or political, tend to idealize one aspect of the work of the Holy Spirit. The question of the enduring form of the relations of man with God is not faced, and the result in the end is not unity but division. A particular experience—the solidarity of a liberation movement, speaking with tongues, the response of the believer to baptism, conversion in an ecumenical conference—becomes the absolute by which the faith of others is judged. This experience, congealed in doctrine and institutionalized in a church or mission organization, becomes a new sect, less open to its own transformation by the Spirit than the world or church it set out to change. Orthodox Christians have seen this happen through many Protestant missions in their own countries and have reason to resent it. Father Jean Meyendorff is right in sounding a warning, as he did to the Faith and Order Commission meeting in Louvain three years ago, against the search for unity on a human level in "various social causes, most of them justified and valuable, but still peripheral to the main issue of Christian faith—the ultimate and eternal destiny of man." Metropolitan Nikodim, in the article mentioned above, is realistic in pointing out that the unity of Christians belongs to the whole integral body of the Church catholic; it is not something we possess in an experience here and there. Evangelical Christians eventually must face the same questions about the form of the church, its enduring qualities in this world, and its holiness in relation to the relativity and sinfulness of human institutions, that have beset Christendom from the days of the Greek fathers. They too, in their way, must find catholicity.

When this has been said, however, it is no less true that evangelical ecclesiology bears witness to a reality about the Church to which the undivided church of the New Testament and of the Greek fathers also bears witness and which must be continually rediscovered if the church is to be truly catholic. The church is not a Platonic form, not a static essence of eternal reality above the temporal flux. It is, to use Fr. Meyendorff's words, an eschatological event as it is expressed in the liturgy and the Eucharist. It is the sphere of the action of the triune God in history. Its tradition is, to quote Fr. Georges Florovsky, "'the witness of the Spirit; the Spirit's unceasing revelation and preaching of good tidings." Or, as Prof. Nikos Nissiotis has said it:

> In the church life the personal communion in the being of God is creating the unshakable reality of the ecclesia, communion realized in time. The highest goal of ecclesial being is to be found in St. Paul's verse, "For now we see through a glass darkly, but then, face to face" (1 Cor 13:12). This "face to face" is given in the Greek text by means of a grammatically strange expression, *"proeomen pros prosopon."* This triple use of the preposition *pros* signifies the movement inherent, through creation in all rational beings. A rational being is personal; that means that

he is in continuous movement toward other personal beings through whom he can become aware of his own person. In this way, through the revelation of God in Christ and in the ecclesia, we sense and represent the origin and the goal of the whole creation.[4]

This action, this movement, this history moving toward communion among persons and toward the fulfillment of creation through the drama of God's action in Christ is, if I am properly instructed, what takes place in the divine liturgy. The Eucharist itself is the reality of the event of the life of the triune God in this world for its redemption. Whenever it loses this evangelical character, when it becomes only the ceremony of a self-contained hierarchical institution existing comfortably alongside an unredeemed world, it breeds evangelical protest against itself. Here is where our dialogue must continue to search the integrity and fullness of each other's witness and none of us can take refuge in a self-justifying ecclesiology.

2. Different, but analogous, is the tension between Orthodox ecclesiology and that of the churches of the Lutheran and Calvinist Reformation. The Reformation belief in an *ecclesia semper refornlanda*—a church always being reformed—is a continual source of confusion to our fellow Christians both Catholic and Orthodox. Either it sounds to them like a version of event or experience ecclesiology, or like a contradiction. Metropolitan Nikodim understandably takes exception to a sentence in Dr. Eugene Garson Blake's report to the Central Committee of the World Council of Churches: "The way for the World Council of Churches to serve the ecumenical movement in our time is to become as radical an influence for a revolutionary new obedience to Jesus Christ as we must be a conservative force to preserve for the world the ancient Gospel of the transcendent God who makes himself known in Jesus Christ, 'his Son our Lord.'" This is not ecumenical ecclesiology. I hear the Metropolitan saying in more polite words; "This is Reformed double-talk, which on its revolutionary side slides over into a dissolving of the church."

No Lutheran or Reformed church can deny that this danger is real, beset as we are by biblical literalists on one side, charismatic movements on another, and revolutionary crusades on a

---

[4] *Theology Today*, 1962.

third. Yet we live with faith and hope with this danger because the central experience of the church for those in our tradition is that of a community of corrupt and sinful human beings who are continually being forgiven, united into one community and sent to be witnesses in the world by the one God, Father, Son and Holy Spirit, who acts among us in word and sacrament. In the sense of being continuous with the undivided church of the first centuries, this is event-ecclesiology. "Where the gospel is rightly taught, and the sacraments rightly administered," reads Article 7 of the Augsburg Confession, there is the church. This is an objective reality which does not depend on human experience or the qualities of human fellowship. It is furthermore a continuing reality through history, a living tradition governed by the authority of divine self-revelation in Holy Scripture but expressed in the wholeness of the witness of the church, both in the East and in the West and today in continents and cultures which yesterday did not know Christ. In a sense, the Reformation moved away from the specific Roman Catholic concept of hierarchical authority defining the church toward the Orthodox spirit of *sobornost*. The continuity of the church lies not in the legal transfer of power from bishop to bishop but in the whole body which expresses itself in gathering for worship, in its orderly and constitutional synods and councils, and assemblies.

Nevertheless, the difference between Reformation and Orthodox ecclesiology is not profound and real, nor have we fully plumbed its depth. It lies in the Reformation understanding that the church is at one and the same time the body of Christ and a community of sinful human beings responding imperfectly to the grace of God. This understanding affects worship, order, sacrament and witness at every point. This is why the church confesses its sins in every worship service, and especially before partaking of the Lord's Supper, and why no minister can forgive sins but only make known the forgiveness of God. It is why Protestant church order hedges every authority about with constitutional limitations and places all major decisions in synods and assemblies where, in free debate, brothers and sisters may inform and correct each other in the word. It is why Reformation churchmanship is profoundly suspicious of sweeping and undebated unanimity in moral pronouncements about world liberation, justice and peace, from whatever source they may come. Because the embodiment of Christ is real, and because we sinful human beings are nevertheless its members, there can be no perfect expression of the life of the church in this world, whether in liturgy, theology, hierarchy, social witness, mission or ecumenical movement. At every point in every place, the church is a worldly body whose diseases are being healed and whose misbehavior is being corrected by its head who is Christ. It is being joined together, growing into a holy temple, upbuilding itself in love (Eph 2:21; 4:16). It is the body of Christ but its various expressions can only bear witness to him by the way in which they are being transformed, corrected, or perhaps overcome by his work and presence. In this sense, the Reformers spoke spatially of a hidden and an open, an invisible and a visible side of the one Church of Christ, and temporally of a church, in the tradition of the apostles and all the saints through the ages, always being reformed.

The problem of this ecclesiology is clear, even to those within it. Where does one go for absolute assurance? What can one grasp and hold in times of suffering, of persecution, and above all in situations where the whole pressure of society works on one's inner doubts about the reality of the triune God? Of what tangible visible reality can one say, this is, without spot or wrinkle, the presence of Christ? The Protestant answer is to reverse the question: Christ himself coming to us in his transcendent grace is more real and more reliable than any human construction, even the construction of a divine liturgy or a church hierarchy. When our confidence in all things human fails, he is there. He gives us confidence to live with relative and sinful institutions in hope, knowing that he works through and redeems them. For many Christians this is not an adequate answer. But is it not at least a question for all? Even Orthodox theologians affirm that there is much in the life of the church which needs reformation. Might we not, at this point, get beyond the assertion of our difference on this point in general terms, to ask what, concretely, should be reformed even in Orthodox perspective, and what is constant in the tradition of the church which even Reformation Christians acknowledge? None of us would deny that affirmation of Christ's presence in the church is the basis for any critical or reforming stance. None of us would disclaim that this presence is entirely of his grace and of our works. Have we not, here also, more to learn from each other's experience of the church?

3. My third illustration must be briefer. The Roman Catholic experience of the church has always posed to both Protestant and Orthodox the critical question of authority in both doctrine and order. Both of our traditions have rejected the Roman Catholic answer: one earthly hierarchical organization with one head, authoritative in matters of faith and doctrine, combined with a clear structure of authority and centralized decision-making which can both restrain and legitimate change. But here most of the entire ecclesiological frontier seems to be opening to influences both ways. During the past fifteen years, Roman Catholicism has been through a ferment with regard to its sense both of authority and churchmanship too profound and extensive to be described in a few words here. The character, if not the fact, of papal authority is being reworked. The role and authority of the priesthood is subtly changing. Dogmatic and moral theology is becoming more various and more ecumenical. On the other hand, we all face together the question to which the traditional Roman Catholic position was one answer: Where is the ultimate authority in matters of Christian faith and morals, and in the order of the church? When controversy arises, how can it be resolved? How does the church discern the mind of Christ in a changing world? How does the church distinguish true patterns of response to him and participation in his work? There is urgency to this question today which underlies the ecumenical movement. It comes from the fact that all of us are forced to define and redefine our faith in the face of increasing challenges and missionary opportunities as the world becomes more closely bound in an interdependent system.

What then should we be doing on the way toward the unity which Christ intends for his church? How can we broaden and deepen the consensus we are able to reach in meetings between church leaders and theologians, as his Holiness Patriarch Pimen has urged us to do, so that the consciousness of the whole of our churches may be made aware? In his closing statement to our meeting in Moscow, Father Vitaly Borovpy made five suggestions.

I would like to re-emphasize them here and add a few supplementary suggestions of my own.

- We can continue our contacts and formal fraternal visits, carefully prepared and mutually agreed upon, as we have done so far.

- We can convene groups of theologians from the United States and the Soviet Union to discuss certain concrete questions which may become acute for our future cooperation and demand urgent attention.

- We can increase contact between the National Council of Churches in the USA and the Department of External Relations of Moscow Patriarchate by regular and ad hoc meetings for solving interchurch problems.

- We can institute exchange visits by reciprocal invitations, of professors of theology to lecture in each other's countries to students and the clergy.

- We can arrange a regular and effective exchange of information about each other's churches.

Thus, Father Vitaly. Let me add the following:

- We can broaden and deepen mutual participation by church people, lay and ordained, in each other's liturgies and worship services. This would include mutual education in the meaning of this worship.

- We can intercede for each other in prayer before God, as churches for churches, in public worship. Why should not prayers be made in the Orthodox liturgy for the Baptist churches, for Reformed and Lutheran and Roman Catholic churches, and for the World Council of Churches? Why not the same should be done, with special reference to persons and situations, in each of our Protestant churches as well?

- We can draw on our common heritage in common Bible study as we are doing here, not only among scholars and bishops, but among the laity.

- We can learn more of and share each other's church traditions and theologies, not only Basil the Great and Martin Luther, but Komyakov and Schleiermacher, Bulgakov and Karl Barth.

- We can challenge each other to faith and obedience in Christ, according to our often differing concepts of what that obedience requires. We can, in short, refuse to treat each other as curious animals in another habitat, and take each other seriously as fellow Christians with whom we must struggle for a common understanding of the word and will of God for us all.

This brings me to the second reason given by the Patriarch and by Metropolitan Nikodim for ecumenical relations: cooperation in service and witness to the world. Jesus Christ unites the church not only for itself but for the world. On this, I believe, we agree. But how is the world to be understood as the object of the church's mission and of Christ's action? At this point there are profound differences which do not run between Protestantism and Orthodoxy but through both. Let me illustrate with three contrasting positions.

1. "In Orthodox ascetical theology," writes his eminence Metropolitan Ilya in his address to our meeting in Moscow, "the concept 'world' implies parting of the soul with its normal state, its staying outside itself, its falling away from its own nature. It is separation from communion with God." "Friendship with the world is enmity with God" (Jas 4:4). The struggle against worldliness is for the sanctification of the body "that together with the soul, in a transformed entity, (it) is to become a partaker of the heavenly glory!"

   The Metropolitan expresses here a current which runs deeply through all branches of Christendom and is found in the Bible itself. Lutheran pietism and Calvinist Puritanism were both based on it, even though it was the fate of the former to father the modern world missionary enterprise and of the latter to provide spiritual resources for the commercial and industrial revolution. The role of monastic struggles against worldliness in the Roman Catholic traditions is well known. In all of these the reality of Christ's incarnation is affirmed, as is the goodness of creation. But the world is more than this; it is the power of attachment to lesser realities than God, material realities or earthly influence and position. The way of salvation is liberation from the world and the church is the place of ascetic discipline where by the power of Christ, worldliness is overcome.

Thus far the agreement. Let me add only a question about possible difference. How should the world be renounced in our various traditions? What kind of church expresses the contrasting reality and what kind of Christian discipline should it encourage? Let me briefly indicate some areas in which this question might be further explored:

> a. What is the role of monasticism in the church and what is the calling of a monk or a nun? It is clearly different in Orthodoxy and in Roman Catholicism. Protestantism began with the repudiation of this calling altogether and yet we have today Protestant monastic orders such as the Brothers of Taize. What does it mean in this special calling to renounce the world and in this renunciation to serve Christ in the world?
>
> b. What is the place of asceticism—of poverty, chastity and obedience—in the life of the ordinary believer, and what is its purpose? How might it interact with the stewardship of labor and production, marriage and the family, and the responsibilities of free citizenship in a Christian life of witness? How would Orthodox, Catholics or Protestants differ in their answers to this question?
>
> c. What is the responsibility of the church faced with worldly power in the political and economic organizations of our time? How, in our various traditions, should the end to these forms of power be expressed?

2. "The ideal behind the establishment of God's kingdom on earth is not just perfection of the individual personality," writes Archpriest Nikolay Gundyaev, "but perfection of human society as a whole."[5] The church is to build the kingdom in this world by the power of Christ, by working for human justice in the distribution of material and spiritual benefits, in love. In this statement another concept of the relation of church to world is suggested, which also runs through all our traditions. The church embraces the world, participates in Christ's redemption of the entire cosmos, and the building of the heavenly kingdom on earth. The church affirms all forces in the world working toward this end and seeks to work with them and sanctify them. In the United States, we are approaching

---

[5] *Journal of the Moscow Patriarchate* (1974) 6, l. 68.

the bicentennial celebration of the independence of our country with many expressions of this relation of church to world. Many of our scholars have discovered a civil religion in the American experience, an implicit recognition of God's leading in the achievements of our democratic system, our affirmation of equal rights for all people, and the individual freedom of our social and economic system. One of them, Robert Bellah, even discerns in the capacity of the greatest of our statesmen to recognize a transcendent judgment on American life, a reflection of the action of the biblically revealed God of justice and mercy. We will be confronted as Christian churches with the question during the next two years: In what way can we or should we bear witness to the building of the kingdom of God in American society? How is Christ's redemption at work in this part of the world? Our situation in this regard is not unique. The church in many a newly independent nation in Asia and Africa faces the same question with relation to a world whose culture is not traditionally Christian. Churches in socialist societies face it with relation to a dominant ideology which is Marxist.

There is no question here for any of us of merging the church into a form of civil religion. We can all agree with Fr. Meyendorff that if we "understand church unity as basically a Eucharistic and therefore eschatological reality, our attitude will be different from that which considers the church as immanent in the world, so that its destiny is determined by the secular goals of mankind." Fr. Nikolay Gundyaev places the transcendent and the immanent in a delicate balance: "It might be thought, however, that by transforming, renewing and recreating the children of the church, the Holy Eucharist indirectly contributes toward the renewal of the world outside the bounds of the church pale as well. For the renewed members of the church body—by merging into a single common human family in which all are bound together by very close mental and moral influences—infuse it with divine light, with which they have been filled by the holy chalice. The grace-endowed members of the church help to some degree toward the renewal of the world. ---Thus St. John Chrysostom writes, *The bread of God, descending from heaven and giving life to the world gives life to the whole universe.*" (JMP 1974. no.6; 66.)

Still, however; the question remains, How, in our various traditions, does the church affirm the purpose of God for the world and lead it to its true fulfillment? Specifically,

a. How is the transcendence of the church over the world understood? For the churches of the Reformation this transcendence must be critical and prophetic; where then is the blessing and the sanctification? In the Orthodox vision of infusion with divine light on the other hand, where is the note of judgment?

b. How is the immanence of the church in the world understood? What form of Christian involvement in the struggle for peace and justice might be called specifically ecclesiological? In Orthodox terms, how is the perfection of the body of Christ to be related to the relative and tactical moral choices which must be made in achieving a more human world? In Protestant terms, how can the church bear a faithful witness to Christ's reconciliation of the world amid ambiguous issues and choices?

3. "The church," writes Fr. Georges Florovsky, "is more than a company of preachers, or a teaching society, or a missionary board. It has not only to invite people, but also to introduce them into this New Life to which it bears witness. It is a missionary body indeed, and its mission field is the whole world. But the aim of its missionary activity is not merely to convey to people certain convictions or ideas, not even to impose on them a definite discipline or a rule of life, but first of all to introduce them into the New Reality, to convert them, to bring them through their faith and repentance to Christ himself, that they should be born anew in him and into him by water and the Spirit." (*Bible, Church, Tradition: An Eastern Orthodox View*, 69)

With this, a third relation between church and world is brought into focus: the missionary relation. The church is to evangelize the world, to convert it, to bring it into its new and true reality which is Jesus Christ. No Protestant, whether Lutheran, Reformed, Baptist or Pentecostal, could disagree with Fr. Florovsky's formulation of it. But if we take this relation seriously, what form and style of church life does it call for? If this expression of the question sounds too Protestant, let me put it more fundamentally: How can the Eucharist be celebrated evangelistically—so that those outside the circle of faith will understand that what is being offered them is not the cultural bias and perspective of one people, but the ecumenical reality of Christ himself? The answer of the churches of the Reformation to this question is rooted in the repentance and renewal of the church itself as it faces the judgment and transforming power of Christ toward its traditional liturgy and theology and ethics, in a new society where he is at work. Mission is witness to Christ's victory over us and over the world, to the power that makes all things new. But if I understand aright, this missionary dynamic is, in Orthodox understanding, in the liturgy and in the church, for the world. If, as Protestants, we can come to understand more deeply how this missionary for-ness really operates, and if we can demonstrate to our Orthodox brothers and sisters that in missionary repentance and renewal the church is still the church and not some accommodation to the world, we may also in mission find a deeper unity. May God grant us his Spirit in this search.

I came away from this experience with a deep appreciation of the piety of the Russian Orthodox Church. It was expressed differently in Fr. Vitaly Borovoy and in Metropolitan Nikodim but it was the same piety. It was rooted in the liturgical life of the church which was more basic than any theology or any ideology or political hope. It saturated Russian culture and helped that culture survive. I could worship in that church. On the other hand, Communism required a different encounter than that of transcendence, more like that of the Lutheran/Reformed faith that I experienced in East Germany.

Since then, things have changed in both lands. In 1994, the Hungarian Reformed and Lutheran churches held an international conference on "Christian Faith and Human Enmity." Inspired by this, the Russian Orthodox Church invited the churches in the former Soviet Union to a similar conference in Moscow. It was the most ecumenical meeting ever held there. Will Russian Orthodox Church rise to the ecumenical challenge in the post-Communist era, or will it succumb to nationalism? Pray for it.

X. CHRISTIANS ASSOCIATED FOR RELATIONSHIPS WITH EASTERN EUROPE (CAREE)

In my dissertation, I studied Josef L. Hromadka, a Czech Protestant theologian who accepted the Communist revolution and tried to work within it. Thereby began an involvement with the churches in Eastern Europe (the Communist bloc) which lasted the eighteen years of his life and twenty years beyond with his heritage until the end of Communism.

I had written an analysis of his ideas, based on his English writings. I was in China at the time, anticipating the Communist takeover, which most of the Christians dreaded (from experience) and most of the students welcomed with joy (they read illegal Communist literature and rejoiced in its idealism). Then, two years later, I met him.

It was at the Second Assembly of the World Council of Churches in Evanston, Illinois in 1954, where I was attached to Church and Society as a staff member. I climbed into a taxi to go to a speaking engagement, and there beside me was Hromadka. "You wrote an article about me," he said. And we were friends from then on. I sent him my chapter on him in my dissertation, which he found was fair in its exposition, though, of course, he disagreed with my criticisms.

The next encounter was longer-range. Hromadka had formed the Christian Peace Conference (CPC) in 1958. It was an attempt to establish independence from the World Peace Council, in which the Soviet Union was trying to involve the churches of its area of dominance in Eastern Europe. Hromadka wanted a Christian organization for peace which would bridge the Iron Curtain, and would be separate from the political agenda of both East and West. He had support from those in the West who objected to the limited rearmament of West Germany, remembering the Nazi era; and the pacifist churches and organizations who found hope in the fact that the Soviet Union was at least talking about peace. It held its first assembly in 1961 in Prague. I would have gone, but I was working at the time for the World Council of Churches, which was suspicious of it being a rival ecumenical organization which would involve the Eastern churches against the West.

I did go to the Second Assembly in Prague in 1964. The American delegation was composed of pacifists, peace activists (Daniel Berrigan was there) and curious pastors interested in peace. The western European delegation was similarly composed. From the East there were prelates of the Orthodox churches and leaders of other churches in the area, and, curiously, Marxist philosophers, students, and others whom Hromadka had influenced to come. He saw me in the hall at one point, clapped me on the shoulder, and said, "Charles, I hope you are talking to many people." That was his real agenda: peace through conversation between East and West.

Next year, I found myself in the Methodist office to the United Nations in New York, with Carl Soule, its representative and Christian friend of the Soviet Union and Paul Peachey, a Mennonite and Professor of Sociology at Catholic University in Washington. They were persuading me to join them in forming a US Committee for the Christian Peace Conference. They wanted me *because* I was not a pacifist or a friend of the Soviet Union. They wanted me to chair the Committee.

I rode that horse for seven years. Rather it was several horses that had to be persuaded to make a team. There were those, like Carl Soule, who believed the Soviet Union was really for peace and that agreement was possible on Soviet terms. We thought they were naïve, and had to resist their policies. Then there were others, who did not join our effort, who were opposed to any dialogue with the churches in the East, for whom the only true Christians were those in the resistance or in prison.

In between were the mass of Christians caught behind the Iron Curtain who needed friendship and understanding from churches in the rest of the world. These we tried to serve. This we tried to provide them. The Christian Peace Conference was one vehicle. Hromadka was our guide. We trusted him as a Christian despite our differences with his position. As long as he was president of the CPC, we trusted him to include us in the conversation. We nevertheless formed the US Committee *for* the Christian Peace

Conference. I insisted on the word *for* rather than *of* for two reasons. One was to promote contact and friendship between churches in North America and the churches in Eastern Europe. The other was the danger of having a separate Christian Peace Committee promoting a pro-Soviet idea of peace.

Meanwhile, things were developing in Europe. It seemed for a while as if Hromadka had succeeded. In Czechoslovakia, between 1965 and 1968, under his influence, Marxist officials and philosophers talked to Christians. Milan Machovec wrote, *A Marxist Looks at Jesus.* Viteslav Gardavsky went further with a book entitled, *God is not Quite Dead.* A West German Roman Catholic Society, the *Paulusgesellschaft* held a conference in Czechoslovakia in 1966 on the Christian-Marxist dialogue. The Czechoslovak government under Prime Minister Dubcek eased restrictions on the churches and on the society, and welcomed others who promised to build "socialism with a human face." It happened not only in Czechoslovakia. In France, Poland, and even in Italy similar movements were taking place. It looked for a while as if Marxists could modify their ideology and cooperate with Christians in building a more just society than the capitalist one. "Socialism with a human face," was their slogan, and most Christians could accept it.

The Global South also made its voice heard. Many of them had mildly socialist regimes headed by Christians or others or opposition leaders whom Christians supported. Revolution was in the air, in a form which caused the Soviets unease. Their leadership of the revolution, that it happened once in the Soviet Union and that Soviet foreign policy was the revolution, was questioned by the very people they proposed to lead.

The Third Assembly of the Christian Peace Conference in the Prague Spring of 1968 was a mixture of all these. It was utterly different from the first two. Hope was in the air. Hromadka gave a great speech on the Christian faith and its contribution to socialism with a human face. The Minister for Religious Affairs of the Czechoslovakia government was present and explained to all that a new policy would welcome Christian participation, and already had removed restrictions on church life. It seemed to be a new age.

For a few months in 1968, this spirit lasted. Then, in late August, after the World Council of Churches Assembly in Stockholm, the Soviet armies invaded Czechoslovakia. Hromadka was bitterly disappointed. The whole project to which he had given his life and soul had been destroyed. He wrote a bitter letter to the Soviet Ambassador reminding him that he had been awarded the Lenin Peace Prize for his services to peace and stating that only the immediate withdrawal of Soviet troops from Czechoslovakia could partly restore the relationship which had been so promising. It did not happen. For a year, Hromadka tried to rescue the Christian Peace Conference from degenerating into an instrument of Soviet foreign policy. I was with him in the summer of 1969 with A.K. Thampy representing the CPC units in France, West Germany, Cameroon, and India (those I remember, there were more) trying to develop a strategy from the rest of the world to that end.

It was all in vain. In the Working Committee of the CPC in September, the eastern bloc voted unanimously in the Soviet line. They fired Ondra, the Czech general secretary. Hromadka resigned as president, and in December he died.

The funeral was a strange affair. All sorts of people were there. There were Americans. Dean Elmer Homrighausen of Princeton Seminary, who knew him as a colleague, spoke at the service. Hromadka had spent nine years at the Seminary as professor of systematic theology, in refuge from Nazism before and during the Second World War. In 1967, President McCord invited him for a visit and extended the invitation to twenty-seven of his then living students to meet with him and hear him speak. Twenty-six of them came. In the United States, he was much loved.

There were ecumenical colleagues, including those from what we used to call the third world. Hromadka was a friend of most of the leaders in the World Council of Churches. He had been a member of the WCC Central Committee. He was one of a company of theologians who formed the Ecumenical Movement.

There was the Czech Protestant community which was confused and divided. Hromadka had been a minister and leading theologian of the Evangelical Church of the Czech Brethren which owed its origin to Jan Hus in the fifteenth century. There were those who embraced "socialism with a human face" on Christian principles and hoped that it would be realized. There were those who resented Hromadka for his acceptance of Soviet domination and wanted a more nationalist and more western stand. There were those who resisted specific acts on Christian principles and thought that

Hromadka didn't support them (although he did intervene to protect many of his ministers).

Then there were radical friends, Marxists who had been his conversationalists for years and who had shared his vision of "socialism with a human face."

Finally there were the Soviets. They were not in evidence. No prelate of the Eastern Orthodox Church was there. They had, after all, stolen his Christian Peace Conference and caused his death. But their agents were there, Czech and Eastern European. We were warned about certain people who were untrustworthy. The atmosphere of the funeral was overlaid with suspicion.

We, in the United States, struggled for three years with the Christian Peace Conference. Then we decided that our mission was broader and the Christian Peace Conference, without Hromadka, was not our only channel to the churches in Soviet dominated Eastern Europe. In 1972, we changed our name to Christians Associated for Relationships with Eastern Europe (CAREE). With this name, we pursued our ministry through many channels.

It was twenty years before Hromadka's name came up again. It was on his 100th birthday, in 1989, that the churches in Czechoslovakia felt free enough to organize a conference on his thought. I don't remember what I said on that occasion, but I remember the atmosphere. It was spring. Snow was still on the ground but crocuses were peeping through the snow. It was a promise of things to come. A year later, demonstrations brought an end to Communist rule.

In 1990, a CAREE meeting was held in Princeton in which Mrs. Hromadka was present along with several of his former students. I wrote an article on that occasion which makes a fitting conclusion to the significance of Hromadka for the future. I close with it here.

XI. JOSEF HROMADKA AND THE WITNESS OF THE CHURCH IN EAST AND WEST TODAY[1]

1. A New Era

Let me begin with a statement that sounds standard but is overwhelmingly true: In the year 1989, we stand on the threshold of a new era in the relation of the world's peoples to each other. A new drama, long in preparation, is beginning. The remarkable changes in the Soviet Union under the leadership of Mikhail Gorbachev have raised the curtain on it and we find ourselves in a new history of forces and ideas. Let me illustrate:

a. The political power balance by which we have measured everything since World War II is softening and breaking up. More than that, a new conception of the relation of power to national interest is emerging. Stockpiles of strategic weapons are still there. Military minds in the United States and the Soviet Union continue to press the logic of deterrence and security. But diplomatic initiative lies elsewhere, in radical proposals for disarmament, in a shift of emphasis from defense to industrial technology and trade, and in a discreet cooperation, coping with the trouble spots of the world.

b. The ideological front is breaking up, despite the protests of hard-line Marxists-Leninists on the one side and free enterprise dogmatists on the other. Marxism is open to reinterpretation and criticism in its central tenets. Socialism is being redefined. Class solidarity and revolutionary power are being called into question. All this leaves us and the rest of the world scrambling for new concepts and movements with which to deal with greedy and oppressive powers, and express human hopes for a more just and free society.

---

[1] Presidential address delivered at the meeting of the Christians Associated for Relationships with Eastern Europe (CAREE) in October, 1989.

c. Economic forces at work in this world are out of control. No agency—national or international—is able to call them into account. No world planning can give them effective direction, and only the blindest dogmatists believe that world market forces will solve the problems they create. Bureaucracies are ineffective, even when backed by state power, as the breakdown of socialist economies in Eastern Europe demonstrates. But they are equally ineffective when composed of international bankers, business executives, or UN officials. Meanwhile, the world debt crisis threatens catastrophe unless it is controlled. The gap between the world's rich and the world's poor grows greater, and transnational corporate entities concerned primarily with feeding themselves roam the earth like dinosaurs.

d. Our technological exploitation of God's non-human creation is out of control. In a few cases such as the international treaty limiting fluorocarbon emissions to protect the earth's ozone layer, an extreme and obvious danger has produced universal agreement. But the world's rainforests are still being destroyed. The oceans are still being overfished. Long-term changes in climate are still being produced by atmospheric pollution. We have not solved problems of toxic waste disposal. One could go on. Socialist and capitalist societies have wrestled with these problems and none has as yet controlled them. Marxists, process philosophers, technocrats and environmental idealists as well as Christian theologians, have tried to project a guiding concept of human life in balance with nature, but none has yet captured the allegiance of technological power or human ambition.

e. Meanwhile in the absence of unifying ecumenical visions of world peace and justice, plural loyalties are knitting human community together around alternative centers, and are tearing it apart. This tendency has its creative and its destructive side. Culture, community, and sense of mutual responsibility for the common good are rooted in nations with their common language, their kinships, and their sense of solidarity. Yet racism, xenophobia, imperial domination, and violent conflict are as well. What is a nation? What are its rights? And how are they related to world justice and peace? In a time when the solidarity of the oppressed poor in struggle for world liberation has proved to be a myth and when the promise of universal prosperity through the operations of a world free market system has also betrayed us, we need new visions of community, both national and ecumenical.

We are on the threshold of an era with tremendous possibilities. It is no less than earlier a time of crisis. The historical forces at work here, though otherwise deployed, are rooted in the long history of the last two centuries. We are confronted in them today, as before, with the question of the judgment and grace of God at work in human events and the calling of the church to be God's servant and witness in their midst.

2. The Importance of Josef L. Hromadka

The year 1989 is also the 100th anniversary of the birth of one of Princeton Seminary's great theologians of the past generation, Josef L. Hromadka. Josef Hromadka was born in the small Moravian village of Hodslavice, then part of the Austro-Hungarian Empire, in 1889. Trained as a theologian in Vienna, Basel, Heidelberg, and Aberdeen, he was ordained in 1912 and became a chaplain during World War I. When Czechoslovakia became independent after that war, he helped to create the Evangelical Church of the Czech Brethren and became one of its first professors of theology. Theologically close to Karl Barth, politically a socialist and a Czech nationalist, he was forced with his family to flee his country when it was invaded by the Nazis. From 1939 to 1947, he was professor of Theology and Ethics at Princeton Seminary. Then he returned to his native country as professor in the Comenius Theological Faculty in Prague, there to play a leading and controversial role as theologian and diplomat in his own church, in the World Council of Churches, and in the Christian Peace Conference of which he was the founder. Through his friendship with Marxist leaders, he was influential in establishing the spirit of the "Prague Spring" in 1968. He died in 1969, a year after the Soviet invasion of Czechoslovakia crushed the liberal reforms which he had been so influential in cultivating.

Why is this man, prominent as he was in his own time, so important for us today? I think for three reasons.

First, he was a leader in whom the East and the West combined. With Slavic sympathy, he experienced the drama of Russian history as his own. He probed the depths of human nature and Russian culture with Dostoyevsky. He experienced the Russian Revolution as an event in the life of his world. At the same time, he was a man of Western culture, a Protestant in the tradition of the Czech Reformation, trained in Vienna, Basel, Heidelberg, and Aberdeen, steeped in the spirit of free critical inquiry, political democracy, and personal response to the word of God in the church. His mind is not a fascinating alien world to explore, as is that of Nicholas Berdyaev for example. Nor is he part of a Western world caught behind the Iron Curtain, as are many of the articulate creative theologians of the Evangelical Church in East Germany. In Hromadka, we find a man of two worlds, united in one spirit.

Second, Hromadka's theological task is also ours: to place the history of the world in the context of the word and act of God made known in the biblical story and in the life, death, and resurrection of Jesus Christ. He was a servant of the living God, a witness to the reality of God's kingdom in his situation as we are called to be in ours. Our lives are in the same context of reality known by faith. It is our worlds that differ somewhat. We can learn from him, therefore, in a special way, different from the way we learn from our Western theologians, how to hear the word of God, how to live with Christ, how to be the church, and how to hope for the world.

Third, Hromadka has posed more sharply than any other theologian I know, the question of the meaning of secular historical events in the context of the providence and the promise of God. We may or may not agree with his historical perceptions. I for one have taken sharp issue with him at times. But in all his thought and action, he was a Christian witness. Never were the judgment and grace of God absent from the events and powers of human history; never was the saving promise of God absorbed into these events. We need to learn this art from him today and practice it ourselves. Let me say a few words more about each of these.

3. The Crisis in East and West

Josef Hromadka was a man in whom two worlds combined. It would be more accurate to say that he was a central European who allowed all the social and cultural forces, all the historical catastrophes of his world to work within his soul. The result was a sense of reality expressed so well in the title of his English book, *Doom and Resurrection.*[2] It was a reality he experienced in many ways. As a

---

[2] Josef L. Hromadka, *Doom and Resurrection* (Richmond: Madrus House, 1945).

Czech Protestant in the Hussite tradition, he belonged to a church that had been crushed in the seventeenth century, lived in persecution, flourished again in modern Europe until the new suppression under communist rule. In what reality does such a church live, hope, and bear its witness? He was also a child of the old Austro-Hungarian Empire. In his autobiography, he bears eloquent witness to the spiritual-psychological community which the peoples of that Empire had shared for centuries. The Empire fell and in its place the Czechoslovakian nation arose with its own spirit and its liberal democratic institutions, led and inspired by the philosophy of its president, Thomas Masaryk. This nation was crushed by Hitler, betrayed by the Western powers, and when it rose again was caught in a Communist revolution. How does one make spiritual sense of such a history and how does one live responsibly and with hope in such a world?

Hromadka's response was to draw on a sense of the human drama which was profoundly Russian. Nicholas Berdyaev describes it as "maximalism," a perception of the total demand of holiness on human life and society, an impatience with skeptical criticism, relative analyses of better or worse, and the calculated contracts of bourgeois liberal society. The obverse of this spirit is a profound sense of the demonic at work in human nature, in culture, and in politics, and of the catastrophe to which it leads. Hromadka's mentor was Dostoyevsky, an intensely personal prober of the depths of human depravity, in a world without reference to eternal truth and love, and of the witness of the suffering Christ therein. Like Berdyaev, Hromadka discerned in this the pattern and fate of a whole culture, expressed finally in the victory of the Bolshevik revolution. Unlike Berdyaev, he found the same pattern in the world west of the Pripet Marshes. His appreciation of Thomas Masaryk's understanding of the crisis of Western society as reflected in the history of Russia, and his final rejection of Masaryk's idealistic humanist religion and democratic politics, illustrate this. So does his affirmation of the early Karl Barth's theology of crisis. The message from all of them is the same. In Hromadka's own eloquent words:

> The crisis of our civilization is deep, deeper than any of us are prepared to admit. The civilization as it existed prior to 1914, and, in a way, until 1930, is gone. The cathedral of common norms and ideas, standards and hopes, disintegrated from within. The present world war manifests in an unparalleled way the destruction of

> the (certainly imperfect yet real) unity on which the community
> of the civilized nations had rested . . . We are living on the ruins
> of the old world both morally and politically. Unless we under-
> stand this state of affairs, we cannot help groping and stumbling
> at noonday as in the night. All is literally at stake. No one single
> norm and element of our civilization can possibly be taken for
> granted.[3]

The old order is gone, destroyed by its inner moral decay and by human depravity. The bourgeois liberal order of the West is weak, self-centered and self-indulgent, without the discipline of relation to a single ultimate truth, to a united spirit, and unable to call forth the sacrifice necessary to build a new society. The Communist revolution in the Soviet Union is spreading not only in Europe but throughout the Global South driven by its humanist self-confidence, the devotion of its believers, and the power of masses of poor downtrodden humanity. Through all of this and behind it, the God of judgment and mercy, the crucified and risen Lord is at work. Before this Lord, no halfway measure will work. In his words: "Once the walls between the twentieth century and the days of the prophets and the apostles became transparent, once the distinction between yesterday (Abraham, the prophets, Jesus Christ) and today became impossible, the theologians of crisis grasped the awful 'no' between God and man, were crushed by the burden of human helplessness, and only then, in the hell of mortal fear and nakedness, on the deathline of human existence, they were overwhelmed by the divine 'yes.'"

Is the historical crisis this ultimate? Should Dostoyevsky and the Russian revolution be our guides in understanding it? Has Barth's theology of crisis been drawn here into a basically Russian Orthodox apocalypticism which is contrary to its true message? Does the total surrender of the sinful self to God in faith imply the total surrender of a sinful society to the new forces of history?

4. The Faith of the Church

Josef Hromadka was an evangelical theologian. There is a tension in his thought, I believe, between the sense of total crisis which we have just examined, and the evangelical theology, rooted in Jan Hus and the other reformers, of which he is one of the greatest twentieth century expounders. To this, four points should be made.

---

[3] Hromadka, *Doom and Resurrection*, 118-19.

First, in his theology of crisis the tension comes closest to being resolved. Hromadka, like Barth, clarified his awareness of the living word of God by struggling with the liberal religious thought—in his case that of Troeltsch—of his time. Barth, like Hromadka, was driven by the deepening social crisis of his time—in his case the failure of socialism and Christianity alike to transcend nationalisms of the First World War—to ask with final seriousness the question of a truth which speaks to human beings from beyond themselves. "What is going on at the precise point where the personal, vertical challenge of the living God cuts across the very existence of our personal life?" asks Hromadka, interpreting Barth. "What does it mean that God, *the God*, and not our *idea* of the Prime Cause, not our *idea* of the Universe, encounters us and demands a personal inescapable life and death decision? A decision *Hic et nunc* at the present moment, a decision that cannot be shirked or delayed and postponed? These are the central questions of theology."[4] "Just as the word of God is an event," he wrote elsewhere, "so also theology as an action of thought, is an action of decision, extending hands, receiving gifts of grace and marching to the point of final destination."[5] It is the word of the living God which calls us to listen, to obey. In this revelation knowledge begins. In this reality, we live by faith and from it we understand our world. For Hromadka, like Barth, God's living word destroys every other basis of human self-justification in culture, in religion, in ideology, or in political systems. We live by grace alone.

Second, this gracious word of God is not only over us but with us in Jesus Christ. "In Jesus of Nazareth, God himself has done and does now his work of salvation."[6] He is the reality of our human life. He conquers the powers of darkness in the world including our own sin and therefore sets us free.

> He is the final authority before whom each of us must answer for our deeds. He, the lowly, the scorned, the rejected and the damned one, has gone through death to life, through hell into the glory of God to prove that nothing was hidden from him, that he knows the human way from cradle to grave, from paradise to hell, that he knows what hunger, thirst, sin, guilt, disability and powerlessness

---

[4] Hromadka, *Doom and Resurrection*, 91-92.

[5] J. L. Hromadka, *Theology between Yesterday and Tomorrow* (Philadelphia: Westminster Press, 1957), 25-26.

[6] J. L. Hromadka, *Das Evangelium auf dem Wege zum Menschen* (Berlin: Evangelische Verlagsanstalt, 1961), 132.

> are . . . The whole ladder of physical suffering, social injustice, moral corruption, and the violence of the powerful, was known to him . . . He knew the breadth of human life in its glory and its shame not only as an acute observer. He knows it as one who was fully part of human life, as one who took personal responsibility for it all. His glory did not begin with his resurrection and ascension. His glory, his power, his victory are clear to the eye of faith precisely in the places and moments of darkness, disability, curse and death.[7]

Third, the church of Jesus Christ is rooted in history, but it is the biblical history of the covenant calling of God and of the life, death, and resurrection of Christ, not the history of worldly power, national aspirations, or even revolutionary movements. "The church is not at home under any political regime, nor under any social and economic order."[8] It lives in the world as the gathered community of those who are free to be for the world in Christ because they do not depend on human powers or worldly goods. "The church as the community of pilgrims has to be always on the way, resisting any danger of petrifaction and institutionalism."[9] In its freedom from the world, it is the servant of the world, as it shares the servanthood of Christ to all who are in need while it points the world beyond itself to the justice and mercy of God. The church participates in the struggles of the world for freedom and justice, behind and in which God is also at work, but always with a message of critical prophecy and redemptive servanthood.

Fourth, the church lives in expectation of the coming of Christ into his kingdom and therefore inspires the world with an everlasting hope, always relevant to but never exhausted by human achievements. The promise of God works in the midst of historical events judging, redeeming, and transforming them. The kingdom of God transcends human achievements and infuses the world with hope despite the betrayal of its secular visions. Christians hope for the movements and peoples of the world more than they can hope for themselves, by relating them both to the judgment and to the saving grace of the triune God.

All of this is standard evangelical theology in the Reformation tradition. For Hromadka, however, it had a special meaning. It was

---

[7] Hromadka, *Das Evangelium auf dem Wege zum Menschen,*179.

[8] J.L. Hromadka, "The Church of the Reformation Faces Today's Challenge," in *Theology Today*, vol. vi. no. 4 (January. 1950), 449.

[9] J.L. Hromadka, *Theology Between Yesterday and Tomorrow*, 44.

gospel for human beings like himself and his compatriots, caught up in despairs and the utopian visions, the sufferings and the coercive powers, which multiplied in the upheavals of his world. It meant distinguishing month by month and year by year between a human word—even a religious word—of compromise with the power of the state or of comfort for sullen opposition and withdrawal, and the word of God. It meant discovering new forms of servanthood and sacrifice in a society where bearing the name of Christian was already a stigma. It meant practicing in the church both transcendence and involvement under a government which welcomed only an irrelevant form of one and a conformist form of the other. It meant counseling and inspiring with hope people caught in two forms of despair: some over the loss of the humane culture they once treasured, others over the betrayal of the revolution by its leaders. We have a great deal to learn from all of these experiences for our own Christian witness.

5. History, Judgment, and Promise

"Looking history in the face," or being "confronted with raw history" were among Hromadka's favorite expressions. It was clear that for him the Bolshevik revolution in Russia was the first and remained the paradigmatic expression of this history. Looking back in old age on his reaction to that revolution in 1918, he put it this way:

> Beneath all the horrors, cruelties and brutalities of the revolution and the onset of the civil war, I heard an ominous but clear cry that the division of the world into central European theocratic empires and Western liberal democracies was not the last word. There is a far deeper, an abysmal division between poor and rich, between those who have economic and financial power in their hands and those who have only empty hands or educated heads. This division pervades the whole world, characterizing both victors and vanquished. That which we call the class struggle is not just a propaganda slogan or a cheap call to action. It embraces the most serious of human problems: the fight against poverty and hunger, against the humiliation and exploitation of men and nations.[10]

There was no doubt in his mind that Soviet Communism with its outreach in Communist parties throughout the world was

[10] J. L. Hromadka, *The Impact of History on Theology: Thoughts of a Czech Pastor* (Notre Dame: Fides, 1970), 28.

the vehicle of this struggle. "Communism is not only a doctrine, a theory or a political conviction," he wrote in 1945 to his own Czechoslovak people.

The Communism that we are speaking about today is a revolutionary historical phenomenon and a complicated trend in social life. Communism means the Soviet revolution and Soviet Russia. Communism means the workers' movement based on the Marxist program. Communism means a particular philosophy, Marxism, scientific socialism, and dialectical materialism. Communism also means the Communist political parties in Russia, China, in our country, and in many others. Communism is also the dynamic which is so hard to define in contemporary history, something that is in the air, something which—in human terms—feels like an uncontrollable striving to prevent the broken world from being built up on personal advantages, interests, profits and privileges, but rather on social equality, security and the collective cooperation of the masses of the people. Communism means the partly obscure, partly clear awareness that the countries and nations which bore the responsibility for the leadership and organization of the world order until 1938 are neither morally nor politically able to master the enormous international tasks after the war.[11]

Marxist-Leninist Communism was, for Hromadka, not primarily an ideology but a historical movement carried by disciplined, dedicated believers, with a systematic well-balanced philosophy guiding its policies, empowered by the will and the hope of masses of people "for a social system in which all class differences would fade away, the demonic, tyrannical power of money and private property would be crushed, and all men and women would be united on the same ground of human dignity, freedom and love."[12] This evaluation defined the context of his ministry and determined his analysis of events, in Czechoslovakia and Eastern Europe, in the East/West conflict and tension, and in the radical social and political upheavals in Africa and Asia, right up to the Soviet invasion of Czechoslovakia on August 21, 1968. He understood the "socialism with a human face" of the Dubcek government during the 1968 Prague spring to be a natural development from necessary coercion

[11] J. L. Hromadka, *Looking History in the Face* (Madras: Christian Literature Society, 1982), 31-32.

[12] *The Church and the International Disorder: An Ecumenical Study Prepared under the Auspices of the World Council of Churches*, vol. iv of *The Amsterdam Assembly Series* (New York: Harper & Brothers, 1948), 129.

and control to more participation and freedom, as the members of society became more mature.

After August 21, there was of course a change. Hromadka saw it as a tragic failure by the Soviet Union and other countries of Eastern Europe, to understand and trust this natural development. "What it concerns," he wrote to the working committee of the Christian Peace Conference in October, 1968, "is the question whether socialism is able to develop creatively and whether it will influence the world community, especially the young and the youngest generation by convincing ideas, moral frankness and political wisdom." As he saw it in retrospect, sterile Marxist dogmatism, administrative pressures, and pure power politics were stifling the creativity of the movement. "New socialist orders were created, the socialist house was built. However . . . we were not able to inhabit it by the socialist man." The struggle as he saw it at the end of his life would be for a democratic socialism. "For us there is no way back to bourgeois society. Our state will remain socialist in the full meaning of that word. But we desire to fill it with all the great spiritual and cultural values of freedom, equality and true humanism. This is what we are determined to do, ready for sacrifice and, if necessary, for suffering."

What, in Hromadka's view, is the Christian witness in the midst of this history? It takes for him three forms.

First, repentance. The church can bear no credible witness in a Marxist-Leninist society that does not begin by recognizing its failure to perceive and struggle for true humanity, its practical godlessness often proclaimed in the name of God, its identification with the privileged groups in a morally exhausted and divided old society. All of this is set forth eloquently in the opening pages of his tract, *Gospel for Atheists*.[13] The Christian does not draw battle lines, even rhetorical ones, against the atheist, but with him or her hears the word of the living God, shares the service and solidarity of Christ, in the midst of human need and struggle.

Second, a search with the Marxists for an answer to the basic question, what is human and how is humanity to be served and realized? Marxists are radical humanists: one must credit them with deep and real concern for true humanity. "We have no interest in having the Communist give up his goals and plans or his view of

---

[13] J. L. Hromadka, *Gospel for Atheists* (Geneva: Youth Dept. World Council of Churches and World Council of Christian Education. 1965).

the new society. On the contrary, we wish that he may deepen his knowledge of the laws of nature and society and seek appropriate ways to liberate humanity and build relationships without class and race differences in which self-interests will no longer have a place but will be replaced by true solidarity among human beings."[14] Communism is, in a way, an outgrowth of Christianity. "With its philosophical and practical work and its all-embracing dynamics, (it) is inconceivable in countries which have not heard the gospel of a sovereign God who comes down to the dark vale of human life, or which have no conception of the stormy desire of human beings that the external, social, economic and political structures themselves should reflect something of God's gracious justice."[15] In their common concern for humanity, Christian and Marxist meet each other with the question, how this humanity is to be understood and served, each learning from the faith and dedication of the other.

Third, in this context, Christian witness to the Marxist occurs. There is also a call to repentance for the Communist. Beware of new wrongs, "because the wrath of the Holy Lord will also fall on you and your children if you trample wantonly and willfully on the eternally valid laws of justice and truth. Do not boast so much about your victory. Do not consider yourself greater than this: that you are the servants of the people. And above all, do not imagine that your revolution is the final stage in human history. The Lord of Hosts is also Lord over Communism and is already preparing new expressions of life, of society so that they can go far beyond even the best that Communism has to offer."[16]

This is the crux of Hromadka's transcendence of communist-dominated history. Marxism, however useful in its analysis of past wrongs and historical powers, is inadequate because it tries to find the meaning of history in history. "It has no answer to the ultimate questions of human life and of the heart. Human sin and the meaning of human life go beyond economic relations. The Marxists' 'philosophical method' was adequate for them to explain the world; but in order to make the world into a new creation, they needed something which they could only find in the living

---

[14] J. L. Hromadka, *An der Schwelle des Dialogs Zwischen Christen and Marxisten* (Frankfurt am Main: Stume-Verlag, 1965), 63.

[15] J. L. Hromadka, *Looking History in the Face*, 45.

[16] Hromadka, *Looking History in the Face*, 47.

tradition of the faith."[17] Socialism needs this dimension; the realization of it therefore goes beyond Marxist-Leninist philosophy.

6. Questions for Tomorrow

Many critical things have been said about this judgment of historical powers and moral forces in the history of the past seventy years. Thirty years ago, I wrote about the Hromadka-John Foster Dulles confrontation at Amsterdam in the following way: "In the last analysis both men, the extremes of Christian pro- and anti-Communism, think in terms of a faith which is less than the Christian faith, a faith in culture, society and politics informed by a unifying religion which will meet Communism as friend or enemy on its own level. In both, the Christian remains bound not to Christ in the world but to the world of Communist power and pretension itself."[18]

Today, I think that I was wrong about both men. Pushed by the tensions of the Cold War, each was tempted to overstate the identification of his faith with a particular set of historical powers, values, and ideas, but each finally resisted the temptation. The gospel which they both confessed bore witness to the transcending judgment and grace of God over the society in which they took responsibility as Christ's servants and witnesses.

a. They were both undialectical in their analysis, however, and here remains the problem. How does one throw oneself completely into the service of one's neighbor in the world, into the construction of a more just society informed with compassion and inspired by the hope of true community and freedom, and at the same time bear witness to the judgment of God on the inhumanities and the idolatries of that society? How does one bear faithful witness to and within historical power?

This is the first question with which I think Hromadka has left us. His own answer has been profoundly called in question by the events of the last twenty years. Few in Eastern Europe are satisfied today with his picture of Communism as a mass movement for justice, freedom, and community which goes through a period of coercive domination before it emerges into a true

---

[17] Hromadka, *Looking History in the Face*, 50.

[18] Charles C. West, *Communism and the Theologies: Study of an Encounter* (Philadelphia: Westminster Press, 1958),77.

democracy. They have learned too much about the suppression of freedom and the abuse of power in the Communist movement itself. Parenthetically, it might be noted that Dulles' view of the United States giving moral leadership to a democratic world was similarly destroyed by the experience of the Vietnam War. Christian theology needs to make a sharper analysis of historical powers and trends than did either of these men. But most theological leaders have failed in this. Reinhold Niebuhr was more dialectical in his analysis of the power dimensions of human sinfulness in every society, but less helpful in discerning the presence of the risen Christ among the secular forces of the world. Karl Barth was clear about the prior and ultimate reality of Christ in the world but never systematic in relating that reality to historical powers. Latin American liberation theologians have discovered a new divine agent in the self-conscious struggle of the poor and oppressed for their liberation. But this, though helpful in empowering the poor, is in the long run more idealistic and less helpful than Hromadka's understanding of the judgment and grace of God behind and in human events.

How do Christians grasp the work of a just and merciful God in the midst of the political, economic, and cultural changes which are remaking our societies, among social powers that often do not understand themselves? How is power to be diagnosed and made responsible to the welfare of humanity, under the reign of Jesus Christ?

b. A second and related question concerns the Christian vision for society today. For Hromadka and for many others in Eastern Europe and throughout the world, socialism was and remains a relative, secular but real expression of this vision. As an ideal of human participatory community in which all goods are shared, all persons are equally valued and human need has priority over human greed, it seems a normal extension to society of the ethos of the Christian church. But we have watched socialist systems break down during the past few years, failing in the basic task of producing the goods and services which society needs. Meanwhile, capitalists rejoice that their purely secular theory about the laws of the free market seems to be justified by its results. Yet capitalism too, besides its injustice to the poor, faces internal crises. These crises require a degree of social control that would make a mockery of its one claimed virtue: freedom. Neither system, meanwhile, has developed an effective way of living within the limits provided by God's created world. How are justice, freedom, and ecological responsibility to be combined in a viable human society tomorrow? What is the relation of the Christian church to the common search of all humanity for such a society in a world where most ideologies have gone bankrupt? What have we to say to each other out of capitalist or socialist experience about this question, keeping the rest of the world also in our focus?

c. A final question. What is our vision of community in a pluralistic world? For the past century at least, answers to this question have assumed *one* world. This was the message of the free market economists. Karl Marx made it a dogma. Technocratic twentieth century science and industry have reinforced it. In this picture, the world is basically composed of scientists and technologists, producers and consumers, managers and workers, all driven primarily by the desire to control the resources of the world for a better material life.

We are learning in the late twentieth century that this is only part of human reality. Nations are reasserting themselves around the centers of their languages and cultures. Eastern Europe and the Soviet Union offer vivid examples. Religions, not as faiths but as communities bound together by common practices and dogmas, are both uniting and dividing various parts of the world. There is everywhere a thirst for community in a fuller and deeper sense than any ideology can provide. How does Christian faith understand human community as embodied in the church, in the town, in the culture, in the state, and in the world? We should not be complacent. We have not solved this problem in the United States of America. Perhaps we can learn from as well as contribute to the search of nations like the Soviet Union or Yugoslavia for solutions to it there.

In a word, thanks in no small degree to the ministry of Josef Hromadka in his time, we are now no longer groping for mutual understanding across barriers of ideology and deeply contrasting experiences with worldly power. We are in each other's neighborhoods, just as we have always been—by faith and by God's grace in the ecumenical movement—in each other's churches. The problems of the world which we face together in faith are becoming increasingly common. In Christ, we need each other more than ever to face them responsibly and with hope. This, I suggest, is our agenda in the next few years.

XII. SEMINARY YEARS

Princeton Theological Seminary was truly an ecumenical school under Jim McCord's leadership. I remember an Episcopalian, a Lutheran, a Baptist, a Church of Christ minister, and a Roman Catholic, most of whom were still on the faculty at the time I retired. McCord's principle was to search for and find ecumenical Christian scholars of whatever denomination and join them to his faculty. He was at the same time thoroughly Reformed. He took his denomination seriously. I was at home there as an ecumenical Christian, like most of my colleagues. I was the missionary to the faculty and to the students from overseas whom I taught, helping them to understand the Christian faith as relevant to their society, which I understood as being involved in revolutionary action and faith in Christ.

I taught five years with Dick Shaull, a stimulating teacher who had experience in Latin America and was influenced by Roman Catholic liberation theology. At the same time I was asked by Ed Dowey, a professor of Church History, to join his committee that was forming the Confession of 1967. Dowey finally won out. My relationship with Dick Shaull was not renewed after the 1966 World Assembly of Church and Society because he rejected the existing churches in his search for a true church that would live the resurrection. He found it, ultimately, in the Baptist Church in Nicaragua, although I don't think he was satisfied. In any case, I went back to the witness of the Student Christian Movement and the Confessing Church in Germany where I had been educated. I had a different concept of "Church"—more ecumenical and less perfectionist. He was still looking for that church when he died a few years later. I found it fragmentarily in all the churches I visited, including in Princeton but not completely in any of them. Still, the word of God was preached in judgment and in salvation in all of them, as all of the ecumenical statements said and was expressed in the Confession of 1967 of the United Church of which I was a member. All human statements and all human movements may be faithful witnesses in their time and, as such, they must be learned from and respected. But they are witnesses, not the word of God. Even the purest human revolution or the statements of the Assemblies of the Church are subject to change.

The first thing I remember doing after arriving in Princeton was choosing a church. Ben and Louise Anderson, a Black couple, were commissioned as foreign missionaries at the same time we were in 1946 but they didn't go. Instead they found a challenge in this country at the time we were overseas. They were called to Witherspoon Presbyterian Church at the time we were joining Princeton Seminary and encouraged us to attend. Witherspoon was a primarily black church, which was in the process of becoming more ecumenical. It attracted people like us who had missionary experience and others of the Seminary faculty. We felt at home there. Ruth became an elder and our children were active participants in the church community. When, fifteen years later, we moved out of Princeton to East Amwell, we left the church because our children had moved away and it was too far for us to travel. My experience within the Witherspoon family and the close friendships I developed there, as well as the opportunities I had to preach to the congregation, gave me a deep appreciation of the importance of the African-American Church within our community of faith.

In this spirit, I gave myself to a world perspective which was a missionary perspective. My inaugural address at the Seminary was "The Missionary Context of Christian Ethics" and is printed in the *Princeton Seminary Bulletin*.[1]

That describes my calling at Princeton Seminary. I was a member of the Society of Christian Ethics and the American Society of Missiology and I did the same thing in both, namely to discover, as Reinhold Niebuhr and J. H. Oldham did, the form of action most appropriate in a sinful world to follow the judgment and saving grace of the God who came in Christ.

I was primarily drawn to international students whom I found to be concerned in a special way with the relation of God to their cultures. Among them were K.C. Abraham of India, Feliciano Carino and Lester Ruiz of the Philippines, Ruben Alves from Brazil, and Shin Chiba of Japan, all of whom returned as teachers to their native countries.

---

[1] Charles C. West, "The Missionary Context of Christian Ethics," *Princeton Seminary Bulletin* LVIII, no.1 (October, 1964).

Nor was it only a European American point of view. I remember an American student in class asking a minister from Northern Ireland what was really so bad about being a minister in his home country. He answered that he was protected by his profession saying, "You don't shoot ministers." Nevertheless, he always had to be careful for his parishioners. I remember overseas students asking sharp questions about the relation of the Christian faith to their cultures. This was a dimension that most American students lacked. It was part of the missionary experience for Americans.

It was a European American experience which is described in my article on secularization which the European American culture turned into secularism. This discusses the difference between secularism as a philosophy and secularization as a process which is a theological idea.

THE PROCESS[2]

We start with a historical definition. The word "secular," with its variations, "secularism" and "secularization," is relatively new as a general term in our Western languages. Derived from the Latin word "seculum," meaning "age" or by derivation, "this age or generation," its meaning until the nineteenth century was highly specific. Today, in the vocabulary of the natural sciences, it still refers to a long, indefinite period of time which is, however, not recurrent or periodical, as for example "the secular cooling of the earth." In cultural history it was used for centuries to designate those clergy whose ministry was in the "world" as distinct from those who were part of monastic orders. The implication was clearly that the structure and order of the church itself, expressed especially in its monastic life, was not temporal but eternal, whereas the secular realm would pass away. The structure of the medieval synthesis, brought to completion in Thomas Aquinas but deep-rooted in the popular consciousness as well, was not, however, dualistic, but hierarchical. The secular realm was not evil. It was given a certain value and autonomy at its level. It was the realm of temporal political power, of labor and trade, of the appetites in their place, of the natural virtues and the natural law. It was the realm where man seeks his proper

---

[2] This section is an extract from the author's paper on "Community—Christian and Secular" prepared for the World Conference on Church and Society in 1966. A number of the preparatory essays, including this one, were published under the title, *The Church amid Revolution*, ed. Harvey Cox (New York: Association Press, 1967).

ends with the help of his unaided reason controlling his passions. But it was, in principle, a lower realm, the realm of nature not of grace, the realm where reason demands its completion by revelation and where goodness is subordinate to the higher virtues of faith with their structure in the church.

Into this relatively stable world view broke the dynamic process of secularization. The word seems first to have come into use when church lands were turned over to secular princes in the Treaty of Westphalia in 1648. The reality however was already at work, as not only property, but positions of political power, expressions of art and culture, fields of knowledge, and even human ideals and values were gradually removed from the dominance of the church and the sacred structure of ideas and culture it represented. Its expressions were manifold. Already in the late Middle Ages, William of Ockham attacked the concepts of substance, being, and first mover, as categories for understanding nature, and opened the way for later natural science's tendency to think in terms of functional operations. Galileo, himself a believing Christian, sought the right to declare as true a theory of the movement of the earth which his observations suggested and his imagination conceived, even though the entire religious as well as physical world view of his time, was threatened by this breakthrough.[3] The artists of the Renaissance broke through their religious subject matter to express increasingly the vitalities of secular existence in all its variety. Machiavelli, sometimes called the first social scientist, analyzed the political forces of his day to give advice to his prince without regard for any larger structures of philosophy, ethics or religion or for any goal save the unification of Italy. Hugo Grotius, spurred on by the terrible example of the wars of religion, felt it his proper service of God to develop a system of natural law in ethics which would be valid *etsi, per impossibile, Deus non daretur*, for it would be evidently true to all reasonable men, whatever their dogmatic persuasion.

All these examples have one common feature. They did not represent efforts to combat Catholic Christianity with another world view. They were simply movements toward autonomy in various

---

[3] Galileo was, as C.F. von Weizsäcker points out, fighting for a theory which he could not yet prove (*The Relevance of Science* (New York: Harper and Row, 1964, 104-107). His theory, however, was not a new world view, but an explanation of a certain sequence of natural events. Galileo took no responsibility for the philosophical, religious and social consequences of his scientific theory. He demanded for the right to be free as a scientist not to do so.

spheres of thought and life. In most instances Christian faith accompanied, if it did not inspire, them. They were not aware of leading revolution, nor of setting up great new systems of truth. They were trying to solve the relative problems of thought and life which they saw before them, to express the reality they knew. The inherent dynamic of this process is to call in question not only the world view of medieval Christendom, or other forms of Christianized culture, but any sweeping ideology from any source, which tries to organize all of life and thought into one system of meaning and order. This is the world we are a part of today.

CHRISTIANS IN THE *SECULUM*[4,5]

We have described secularization as a movement away from religious world views in theory and away from the dominance of religious institutions in practice. This means, in large parts of the world, a movement away from Christianity and the authority of the church. Those historians have been largely right who have described it as a drama of Christendom, imported in an advanced state of development into cultures which had never known the dichotomy of religious and secular before. But now we must say more than this. Theologically perceived, the proclamation of the Christian gospel is responsible for the dynamic of secularization, and is its first agent. This is so, even when those who carry it have no idea of producing these consequences, because the process begins with the history of the Hebrew people—with the calling of Moses and the revelation at Sinai—and is fulfilled in the incarnation of Jesus Christ and is expressed by the sanctifying work of the Holy Spirit in the church. To put it bluntly, the secularized state of human mind and society can be creative and is full of hope because it is the state into which God calls his people through their relation with him, and in which he sustains them by his grace. It is the attitude toward structures of thought and the common life which is most appropriate to the history and promise of that relationship. It is a quality of faith in

---

[4] *Seculum* (or *saeculum*) is a Latin word denoting a particular period of time or age or generation. For an explanation of how Charles West is using the word, see page 145.

[5] This section is an extract from the author's paper on "Community—Christian and Secular" prepared for the World Conference on Church and Society in 1966. A number of the preparatory essays, including this one, were published under the title, *The Church amid Revolution*, ed. Harvey Cox (New York: Association Press, 1967).

believers and, where faith is not present, it is a condition in which, precisely for lack of any social and metaphysical obstructions, the word of God can be heard most clearly. Let us examine this thesis more closely.

Secularization begins with biblical history. The Dutch philosopher Cornelis van Peursen suggests two forms of man's relation to objective reality which precede: (a) the mythical, wherein man feels himself continuous with the nature and society around him, deriving his very sense of self from his participation in their forms; (b) the ontological, in which being is objective and accessible in its timeless substance to the human reason.[6] Arend van Leeuwen combines them both, on the basis of a comparative study of Hindu, Chinese and early Mesopotamian civilization, into what he calls the "ontocratic pattern."[7] It is pre-biblical, but it is also modern, a temptation and a tendency in primitive culture and modern social science.

From this baseline the biblical history departed, toward a totally new orientation to reality. The story of this is now familiar to biblical scholars and cannot be told here in full.[8] We can only indicate its direction.

1. Man's efforts to lay hold of a structure of being which he himself would control, by grasping it with his mind (metaphysics) or by securing it with ceremonies and experiences (religion) were overturned by the way God revealed himself. One could illustrate almost at random from the Bible. When God first spoke to Abram there was no evidence of mystic illumination or of rational insight into eternal order; rather the content of the address was command, "Go out from your kindred, from your father's house, to the land which I will show you," and promise, "And I will make of you a great nation—and in you shall all the families of the earth be blessed" (Gen 12: 1-2). The God who made himself known to Moses introduced himself historically: "I am the God of your father. . ." and specifically refused to answer

---

[6] Cornelis A. van Peursen, "Man and Reality—The History of Human Thought" in *The Student World* LVI, no. 1, 1963.

[7] Arend Van Leeuwen, *Christianity in World History* (London: Edinburgh House Press, 1964), Chap. IV.

[8] See, for example, Martin Buber: *The Prophetic Faith*; J. Pedersen: *Israel*; G. Ernest Wright: *The Old Testament against Its Environment*, et al. A good summary of the argument is found in Van Leeuwen, *Christianity in World History*, Chapters 2 & 3.

the question about his name, except in historical terms (Exod 3: 14-17).

2. As with the being of God, so also are nature and history reflected in the human activities of economics and science, politics and culture. The biblical basis of human knowledge and action in all these spheres is the relation which God establishes with his people, known as covenant. The biblical covenant is first a personal relation. The reality it reflects is that of the personal claim of another on us as free and responsible agents. But it is also a relation between God and a community of believers through which his relation to the whole human world is expressed; and it is a dynamic, active relation which expresses itself in events to which structures of society and the stuff of the material world are instrumental.

Once again the biblical history is the story of human attempts to capture this relationship in sacred structures of political or natural order, and of God's judgment on the structures which re-establish the community of faith in a properly secularized world. We take three examples which still play a role in our life today.

(a) It is well known that the basic principles and prescriptions of human behavior known as the law play a large part in biblical, as in later Jewish and Christian, history. The laws in the Old Testament, as the prescriptions for Christian behavior in the Pauline letters of the New Testament, are of various kinds. They have borrowed heavily from the codes of surrounding peoples. In some cases they represent improvements on those codes, in others they reinforce the best available morality of the time. In any event they were modified and even reversed from time to time, as historical conditions in the covenant relation between God and his people changed the response required. Ceremonial laws commanded at the time of the Exodus became an offense to the eighth century prophets, as did commandments in modified form for the post-exilic Jews. The Ten Commandments were drastically modified by Jesus; in some cases, as with the law against killing, adultery and covetousness they were given a new dimension; in others, as with the Sabbath commandment and that on honoring parents, they were sharply corrected. The moral law in the Bible, was basically those teachings (*torah*) which expressed for a time and place, the quality of relation which God had given with his covenant and which is made finally clear in Jesus Christ.

In short, biblical history secularizes the law. It also records revolts against this secularization. The book of Deuteronomy records a legal reform whereby the people of Judah hoped to make themselves acceptable to God, only to be told by Jeremiah, "They have healed the hurt of my people slightly saying 'peace, peace,' when there is no peace" (6: 14). The law which Paul rejected was of the same character. His "All things are lawful for me, but not all things are expedient" (1 Cor 5: 12) expresses exactly the congruence of biblical and modern secular attitudes. Law is, and should be, the servant expediency.

(b) The biblical story secularizes nature. It places creation—the physical world—in the context of the covenant relation and does not try to understand it apart from that relation. The history of God with his people has a setting, and this setting is created nature. But the movement of history, not the structure of the setting, is central to reality. Physical creation even participates in this history; its timeless or cyclical character, so far as it exists, is unimportant. The physical world, in other words, does not have its meaning in itself. There are no spirits at work in it which can help or harm mankind. It is the creation of God alone and is the object of his manipulation.

(c) The biblical history secularizes the forms of the community of believers itself. This has been the hardest lesson of all for believers to learn. The people of Israel did not believe the prophets who prophesied the victory of their enemies because God, in their minds, was bound to his temple and to the prosperity and security of the people he had chosen. Even the disciples throughout the life of Jesus were thinking in terms of the kingdom of God as a sacred order which he would bring in: "Grant us to sit, one at your right hand and one at your left, in your glory" (Mark 10: 37). And Paul was at constant odds with the sacralists to whom he himself brought the gospel: "Already you are filled! Already you have become kings! And would that you did reign, so that we might share the rule with you!" (1 Cor 4: 8). Over against all this the covenant shows itself to be an ever-changing relation, the constancy of which lies in the character of God and not in the structure of the community.

The church is the community which cannot escape knowing all this, and which is called first to apply it to its own life. It lives by its participation in the death and resurrection of Christ in the Lord's Supper (Holy Communion, Eucharist). Its worship is a hearing and a responding to the word of God preached in its midst. These two acts give to the church itself a functional, secular existence. Because of them, the church lives by rediscovering itself as judged and renewed by the work of Christ, by the transformation—potentially the transformation of the world—which goes on in its midst.

SECULAR THEOLOGY[9]

This sets the terms of the theological task in modern society. We close with some suggestions on its content and direction.

1. We are left, by the whole history we have described, with the question of the reality of God. We say "reality" rather than "being," "essence" or "nature" in a deliberate effort to avoid the kind of thinking we have hitherto called metaphysical. We mean by it, that long tradition of deductive system building based on the first principles of thought and being, which is associated with the names of Aristotle and Plato, with the Greek church fathers and with Thomas Aquinas, with Descartes, Spinoza and Leibniz, and subjected to basic criticism by Kant. The secular mind and biblical revelation are at one in rejecting the way of thinking which this system building requires, and the understanding of reality which is associated with it. Neither God nor his creation reveal to the human mind the structure of their essential being, for the very idea of such a structure or essence is a product of the human mind and therefore the instrument of man's desire to make his own ways sacred or absolute. The metaphysical task in the secular context then must be differently conceived—as the task of clarifying and relating ideas about man's situation within the limits of a particular position and bias in human history. Its point of reference will not be an ultimate structure of being but

---

[9] This section (except the last three paragraphs) is an extract from the author's paper on "Community—Christian and Secular" prepared for the World Conference on Church and Society in 1966. A number of the preparatory essays, including this one, were published under the title, *The Church amid Revolution*, ed. Harvey Cox (New York: Association Press, 1967).

the dynamic relations of this history and the responses it brings forth.[10]

We know the reality of God only in and through his acts in history, his covenant relation with man, his calling, judging, centrally expressed in the life, death, resurrection and coming again of Jesus Christ. Through these acts and in this relation we know him to be free, sovereign Lord over creation, man and history. The words we use to describe him—just, merciful, loving, and the like—are not definitions, but themselves expressions of our relation, and pointers to a reality which transcends our comprehension. Nevertheless, we know God as truly and wholly present with us, not partially removed into a mystical absolute. "God is who he is in the deed of his revelation," writes Karl Barth.[11]

This reality is differently perceived from most objects of human knowledge. He who acknowledges it lives within it. It lays claim on his actions; he understands himself and his world as part of this history. It is not a doctrine the truth of which he demonstrates, but a relation which he explores with his mind and expresses with his responsible life. For him, "the will of God is what God does in all that nature and men do. It is the universal that contains, transforms, includes, and fashions every particular."[12] He does not comprehend it or control it from God's perspective. He reckons with and depends on it as God's gift.

This is conventionally known as the response of faith. It is not, however, optional for secular man. In his specialized fields of activity, in the variety of his human relations, in the use of the power in his hands and in his free responsibility the question cannot be avoided: What is the character of the reality with which I will reckon here? It is first a practical question. It is answered in the way money is spent—in families or in the budgets of nations. It is answered in the way machines are built and handled, and in the direction of research. It is answered in the way of a man with a woman, in lifelong marriage or passing relation. It may well be that most of us at this level are practical polytheists. Our realities clash and jostle, and we acknowledge them all.

---

[10] I am grateful to Mr. Ian Ramsey for the reminder that such a metaphysical task is possible. Cf, also S.N. Hampshire, "Metaphysical Systems," in *The Nature of Metaphysics*, ed. D.F. Pears (London: Macmillan, 1957).

[11] Karl Barth, *Kirchliche Dogmatik*, II/1, 203.

[12] H.R. Niebuhr: *The Responsible Self* (Harper & Row: New York, 1963), 164.

But it is the most responsible secular man whom this satisfies least, for he is left with the question of the integrity of his human responsibility itself.

There is a law in me or in my mind, the law of my integrity; and there are many laws in my members, the laws of response to many systems of action about me. In my responsiveness and responsibility to the many, I am irresponsible to the One beyond the many; I am irresponsible as a self, however responsible the natural, the political, the domestic, the biological complexes in me may be in relation to the systems of nature, or to the closed societies of nation, church, family or profession, or to the closed society of life itself.[13]

The problem of reality in secular terms is the problem of the one Other to whom I as a whole human being am responsible, in and through the actions I perform and the other responsibilities I bear.

2. We are left with the question, then, of the secular reality of man. Toward this the whole foregoing discussion points. "The being of man is the history," writes Karl Barth, "in which one of God's creatures is elected and called by God, is included in his self-responsibility before God, and in which he shows himself qualified for this call and task."[14] The reference is of course to Jesus Christ. It would be incomprehensible were we to think of God, Christ or man as substances with attributes. In fact, however, it expresses the heart of the dynamic relation of all three. Christ, says Bonhoeffer, is "man-for-other-men." This is his character. It describes the innermost quality which his acts and relations revealed. As such, he revealed also the decision of God to be for man, epitomized the meaning of all the full-bodied terms—holiness, righteousness, mercy, loving-kindness—with which the Old Testament had tried to express this relation. Man then is defined—given his existence, calling and destiny—by his relation to the action of this God in Christ. In this action the whole world is included in its secularity and man is turned toward it as servant and witness by virtue of being "in Christ."

Man exists, then, as Christian faith sees it, in a field of personal relationships at the center of which is Jesus Christ. He is

---

[13] Niebuhr: *The Responsible Self*, 138.

[14] Barth, *Kirchliche Dogmatik*, III/2, 64.

constituted in his very being by his actions and responses in that field. From him we derive our power to be human and our ever-changing understanding, in specific relations, of what it means. Through his work, God negates the power of our inhumanity, releases us from fear of ourselves. And frees us to shoulder responsibility and take action which serves our neighbor, even when we incur guilt thereby. Because Christ is there, man is not an individual, nor part of the masses, nor the creature of a race or culture, nor the citizen of a nation, but a person in these various contexts, free for the responsibilities they carry because he is free from defining himself in terms of them.

3. The question of an authentically secular society receives thereby a theological answer. Society—the political and economic structures of the common life and the cultural habits and values which give it a sense of unity—is a creative task given to man, not a structure to be received. It is a Christian responsibility to help the secular world to remain truly secular when it itself is tempted to lose confidence in itself and to give way to new ideologies or myth.

The church participates with every secular society in its search for justice and freedom for all its people. As this involves social analysis, political action and formulation of the particular hope of that people, it may mean many an ideological risk. But the church and its theology have the task of reminding such a society that its focus is the true need of man, that its function is the cultivation and development of personal relations among its members in free and experimental interaction. They have the task of warning the commonwealth whenever human beings are in danger of being sacrificed to institutions, projects or ideas. They have the task of confronting such a society through the church's own life and thought with the vision of what man is, the purpose for which he lives, in Jesus Christ, and with the continual self-criticism and reform which this involves. The final point will attempt to spell out one illustration of what this implies.

4. In no area of society are the problems of responsible action more baffling or the situation more dangerous than in the sphere of national and international politics. This is partly because power which can destroy the world is located here, but also because it has been so incompletely secularized. Many political ideologies

have lost their convincing power; indeed we owe the precarious peace of coexistence to the fact that this is so. But mythology, especially of the secular religion of nationalism, persists even among those who no longer believe it, and political decisions are made which reflect illusions more than reality. The present writer is an American. What he says will inevitably reflect that country's experience. But it may still be of some more general value to pose the question from one setting: What is a Christian's responsibility for his country's policy?

First, he is called to act as a solvent of the nation's remaining illusions. When several years ago George F. Kennan propounded the thesis that foreign policy must be based frankly on a nation's self-interest, and not on moral principle, he was speaking as a responsible Christian. When a nation sets up its own national morality—even its concepts of freedom, justice and peace—as a universal standard by which to measure others, this self-justification becomes the heart of disobedience to God. In fact, a nation is, like its citizens, a self-interested body, whose insight into the truth about world order and whose morals in working for it, are highly relative. It lives in a world of other such nations with which it must interact. The Christian is called to prepare the nation to see the judgment and calling of God in the give-and-take of world affairs, in the defeats as well as the victories of its policies. As a secular institution, the nation is not absolute. Loyalty to it must be critical and qualified, in order that it may better serve its proper limited purposes, as one expression of responsible community among men.

Second, the Christian is deeply involved in the responsibility which his nation has for using what power is at its command to serve human need. From this responsibility there is no withdrawal without unfaithfulness to God and to one's fellowman. Having said this, however, let us be clear that there is a radical difference between a nation's self-interested use of power and the use of it which God intends. The power of foreign aid and trade is a major example. Christians are in the position therefore of continually seeking to help the nation to reinterpret its self-interest in terms more inclusive of the needs and interests of others, and at the same time holding up the mirror of Christ to all self-interest as a judgment and a stimulus to the imagination.

The nation will always argue that its most creative and altruistic policies are consistent with its self-interest. The church lives from the conquest of its self-interest by the power of Christ, on which the peace of the world depends. By the continual operation of this tension, the policies of the nation are made fruitful.

Third, the Christian, fully involved with his nation's capacity to make war—in this case possibly nuclear war—bears witness to the nation of the relativity of all conflict to the purpose of reconciliation. No nation is righteous enough to seek an unconditional surrender. No cause is just enough to excuse any means of conflict to fight it. Because Christ has brought peace to all men, there are no absolute conflicts or enmities. There are also no absolute governments. It may be that a nation must fight at times for people—its own or others. But then the welfare of the people must be the test of the battle and of the terms on which it ends.

Finally, the Christian recognizes that political power, like all power, has its limits. It can coerce, but rarely heal. It can set limits to human behavior, but rarely win people's allegiance. It can put down rebellions, but it cannot—at least American power cannot—produce a social revolution. Secular reality in politics includes the moment when the most creative political action is to renounce power and to bear witness in defenseless service to the human relations one seeks to establish. There are times—and there are nations which have lived through them—when the only wise political act is to suffer injustice and oppression not in hate but in forgiveness and inner freedom, out of which a new relationship may grow. Here also the pattern of secular reality is the pattern of the Man-for-other-men. Secular men in any situation can see the human logic of this. But that this pattern contains hope, that the future belongs to the reality we find in this man, is a truth for which there is no proof, there is only witness. This is perhaps the irreducible Christian contribution to the integrity of the secular community—to live within it ourselves, in all its incoherent functionality, in all its appalling responsibility for power and for powerlessness, in all its search for particular forms of humanness, as men who see by faith a promise here which is based not on analyses of social trends, but which comes to all of us from without. If we live by the reality of this future, we shall be secular men but we shall not be conformed to "the world," for we shall be looking at it from the angle of its meaning and direction given by that acting reality whom we call God. By the never-ceasing operation of this tension in all who believe, the secular life of the world is made fruitful.[15]

The Hebrew worldview was confused by the dualistic worldview of Plato. Plato assumed a dualistic worldview as distinct from historical perspective. This infected theology with the heaven and hell distinction, perfection and imperfection which has infected the world view ever since. It is Greek and not Christian. It does not accept the future as advent of the coming of Christ. It leads to dualism which most white Americans reflect. Its future is dualistic and not based on expectation, and therefore perfection and not the future coming of Christ. This is a secularist point of view which inevitably leads to the substitution of historical hopes for the nation or the family, church and society, heaven and hell. It is spatial not temporal. This is characteristic of the American point of view, against which the Christian faith struggles. I have described it as a European struggle and have described it more fully in chapter 3. This was brought home to me by my experience of five years in The Ecumenical Institute of the World Council of Churches where denominations and countries met. There were a minimum of eight denominations and twenty countries who gathered as members of the World Council of Churches around certain subjects which were mission and politics but also to get used to one another.

When I returned to this country, I turned to the study of the gospel in our culture. The pluralism of American culture was brought home to me by an attempt to reach out to minority cultures in this country. I had a fair grasp of the secularism of white American culture as distinct from secularization, but I had not touched on the various minority cultures in our country.

During my time with the Witherspoon community, I discovered the true depth of this country's African-American Christian culture. I also became increasingly aware of the various Asian, Latino, and Native American cultures, each of which was trying to adapt to life in the United States of the twentieth and twenty-first centuries. I remember offering a course of the gospel in our culture expecting that there would be primarily white students who would take it. The

---

[15] The extracts from the author's previously published paper in *The Church amid Revolution*, ed. Harvey Cox (New York: Association Press, 1967) ends here.

result was eight Koreans, two persons from Burma and a number of other countries including one white American. I was prepared to change my class in order to accommodate them. I was prepared to ask them how they say they saw their own culture as transformed by the gospel. An interesting perspective developed among the Koreans. The predominant problem was the Confucian culture in relation to the Christian faith. Most of the male students saw it as a problem of accommodation. There was one female student with whom I talked later (she didn't speak up in class) who regarded Confucianism as the major obstacle. There was one student who saw industrialization as a major problem. All of them were trying to adapt to American culture and had difficulty doing so. The problem of most overseas students is to adapt to American culture which they regard as normative for the Christian faith. I had had experience in their countries, so I was able to help them.

I close with an item which forms a fitting conclusion to this chapter and this book.

XIII.   FAITH, HOPE AND LOVE

It has been many years since I wrote for both Ruth and me about the meaning of life including the role which death plays in it. The last one extant was a meditation on John Donne's poem, "Hymn to God in My Sickness" about twenty years ago, as an introduction to our living wills. It still expresses our thoughts, but it needs to be upgraded in the light of the last twenty years of experience in which I have learned many things, and so has Ruth, though I don't presume to speak for her.

The Apostle Paul, in his famous hymn to love (1 Cor 13) says, "Now abides these three, faith, hope and love, and the greatest of these, is love." A bit about each of them:

Faith is the most difficult. It seems contrary to reason. That God would choose such an inconspicuous speck in the universe as the earth to self-reveal, such an insignificant history as the Jews with whom to covenant and in whose life to be incarnate—it all seems irrational. It seems a fantasy of the religious imagination at best. Bertrand Russell said it without illusion more than a century ago: "Blind to good and evil, reckless of destruction, omnipotent matter rolls on its relentless way" (*A Free Man's Worship*, 1903). Nothing scientific reason has discovered since then has given meaning to the universe.

Yet everyone still believes. Everyone has faith in something or someone. We could not live without it. It may be faith in one's own reason, into which we build our morality and our responsibilities. It may be in an ideology, religious or otherwise. It may be in a person whom we trust. Two stories, one from history, one from today, will illustrate.

In the seventeenth century, Rene Descartes, the famous philosopher, found himself in an inn alone and asked himself: "Of what can I be absolutely sure?" He reached the conclusion: "I think, therefore I am." The essence of humanity is thinking, and therefore reason. He was alone; no contact in his mind with other people, no dependence on them for revealing truth. What about God?

Confidence in reason was rooted in the fact that the extension of his mind, his perception, was reliable. God would not deceive him. The human mind is the divinely given instrument with which to measure truth. The subject-object relation, excluding all emotions and subjectivity, produces truth.

It is time for the second illustration. We were sitting with the faculty of the department of philosophy in a major Chinese university. The chairman was outlining the major themes of Confucian philosophy which, he said, was true and could undergird Chinese society. I asked whether everyone agreed. His colleague spoke up. "No," he said, "The issue is not, what is rational, but whom do you trust?" He then described a Christian philosophy based on his faith.

The message of these two incidents is clear. Human beings are not alone. The image of the detached mind is an illusion, as is the situation of being alone with one's thoughts in a French inn. We are in relationship, as the creation story tells us. What is the meaning of that relationship? Whom do we trust to reveal that relationship to us? What, in other words, is the meaning of the natural sciences, history, politics, psychology, and all the rest of the things we study? What motivates us to investigate them? What motivates our life in the world with others? Who are we, as revealed to us by others, by God, by nature, and by our relationship, our dependence on, other persons?

All my life I have been searching for truth with meaning. I studied philosophies, histories, religions and psychologies in this search. I was looking for objective truth, convincing to everybody, but truth with meaning for human lives. I have come to realize that these are incompatible. Faith always involves the risk that one might be wrong. But doubt is not a thing to play with. It challenges a trust by which one lives. We must choose, but we are chosen by the reality that we confess. "Whom do we trust?" is the right question. We cannot trust our reason; it is too captive to our motives, good and bad. We cannot trust our emotions for the same reason. We trust other people; but we understand them as human, and therefore with their own motives, and fallible. Of all the alternatives, I chose to trust God who guided and corrected the Jews, who came on earth in Jesus the Christ and who guides and corrects by the Holy Spirit. That is a second person relation, you not (s)he. Its expression is prayer. I realize I have not sufficiently melded my thoughts with prayer. I have been too objective, too third person, in my relation with God, despite the image of God's love which I have found in Ruth first, and the family later. I hope God will forgive.

In any case this is my faith, with the whole church through the ages. I hope it has guided and corrected all my thoughts. Whether it has guided all my actions, others and ultimately God will judge.

Hope is a consequence of faith. For me, it rests firmly on the rising of Christ from the dead. Sixty years ago, there were signs of hope everywhere in the world. Hitler had been defeated. Europe and Japan were transformed by enlightened policies. The United Nations was formed. Economic development projects for the emerging nations were planned. The World Council of Churches had been formed as partner to the other half of Christianity, the Roman Catholics, in bearing witness to Christ. Only the threat of nuclear catastrophe remained and that was limited by the prospect of mutually assured destruction. We had learned a lesson. The world was full of hope and the Christian hope was a part of it. There were signs of Christ's rising everywhere.

Today shadows of that hope remain, but new problems have arisen. Worldly hope has faded, and fear has taken over. Yet there are signs of resurrection—in the response of people everywhere to the suffering of others. One finds it in the response to natural disasters, in the search and negotiations for peace, in the outpouring of help for those in need, and in the belated recognition of what we are doing to our natural environment and the remedies for it.

Christians pray, "Thy will be done, thy kingdom come on earth, as it is in heaven." Heaven, to which we hope soon to be going, is God's reign, God acting. God is acting in the world today and we discover it and bear witness to it. The communion of saints, living and dead, is active in our world. Whether dead or alive, we are part of it.

"The greatest of these is **love**."

"God is love," says the first letter of John (4:8). All human gifts come to an end. The end may be natural, or it may the result of human behavior. Our love, however well-intentioned, is imperfect. It needs to be completed and corrected by God. But God's love lasts forever. It was with us in our battles. It went to the cross for us. It fulfills our human love and transforms it. That is the miracle that redeems us every day. When I was young, I proclaimed to everybody that in our 60s, Ruth and I would still be married and in love.

Now it is 30 years past that time, and I never foresaw how deep our love could be in our 90s. There is something of eternal life in that experience, that prepares us for the kingdom of God. We are still learning how to love—how God loves—our human neighbors, those who love us, and those who don't.

"Thy kingdom come." We hope we are ready for it. In any case, we count on God's mercy to take us as we are. God bless you all.

Charles